Reading for the Academic World

2

Reading for the Academic World 2

Averil Coxhead • Paul Nation

© 2018 Seed Learning, Inc.
7212 Canary Lane,
Sachse, TX, USA

All rights reserved. No part of this book may be reproduced, stored in a retrieval system, or transmitted in any form by any means, electronic, mechanical, photocopying, recording, or otherwise, without prior permission in writing from the publisher.

Acquisitions Editor: Casey Malarcher
Content Editor: Anne Taylor
Copy Editor: Daniel Deacon
Design: Highline Studio

The authors would like to acknowledge Stephanie Alexander, Kelly Daniels, Andrea Janzen, Michael Souza, and Joy Yongo for contributing material to this series.

http://www.seed-learning.com

ISBN: 978-1-9464-5280-1

10 9 8 7 6 5 4 3 2 1
22 21 20 19 18

Photo Credits
All photos are © Shutterstock, Inc.

Reading for the Academic World

2

Averil Coxhead • Paul Nation

Seed Learning

Contents

Introduction 6

Language
Unit 1   Some Dos and Don'ts 9
Unit 2   Choosing Your Words 15

History
Unit 3   Inventors Who Changed Our Lives 21
Unit 4   Protected by Nature 27

Science
Unit 5   The Elements of Disguise 33
Unit 6   Lights in the Sky 39

Psychology
Unit 7   Make It a Habit! 45
Unit 8   Dancing Until You Drop 51

Literature

Unit 9   Creative Writing ································ 57
Unit 10 Personal Narratives ··························· 63

Business

Unit 11 Office Hours ····································· 69
Unit 12 Management Styles ··························· 75

Music

Unit 13 The Root of Modern Opera ················· 81
Unit 14 The Connection Between Music and Language ·········· 87

Health

Unit 15 An Important Woman in Medicine ········ 93
Unit 16 Is Your Computer Killing You? ············ 99

Introduction

Reading for the Academic World is a three-book series designed for students who are seeking to develop their academic reading skills with particular focus on passages incorporating vocabulary items from the Academic Word List. By employing informative texts from various academic fields including history, natural science, literature, social issue, psychology, business, linguistics, and more, this series exposes students to a wide range of vocabulary and structures typically encountered in written academic discourse while targeting study of more than 500 words featured in the Academic Word List. All passages in the series are supported with activities to practice comprehension of input, refinement of output, fluency with current skills, and language-focused learning strategies.

Each unit of *Reading for the Academic World* contains the following sections and features:

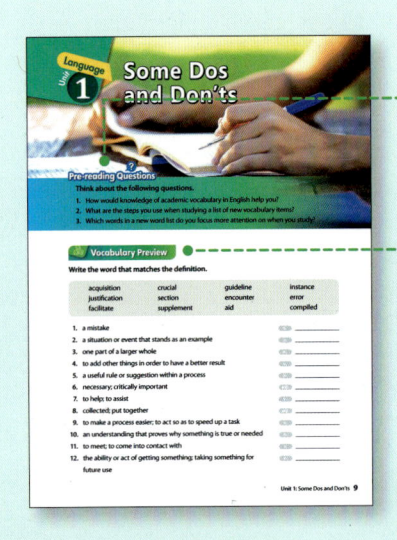

Pre-reading Questions

Three questions are provided here to guide students in thinking about personal experiences or opinions directly related to the unit's content.

Vocabulary Preview

Each passage in the series highlights twelve target items from the Academic Word List. Short definitions help prepare students for the word's particular usage within the context of the unit's reading passage.

Topic at a Glance

A short paragraph introduces the topic of the passage for students.

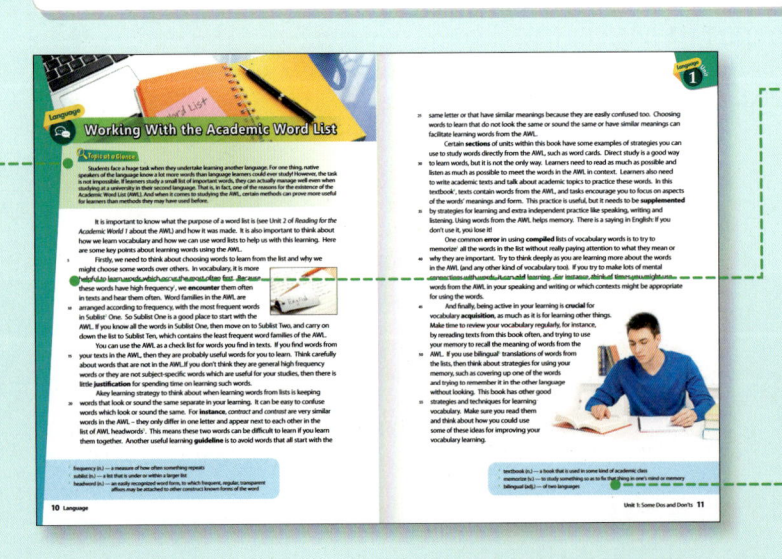

Reading

All passages are written in an academic style and range in length over the series from 600 words to 800 words.

Footnotes

Lower-frequency vocabulary items are defined in footnotes to support comprehension and additional vocabulary development.

Reading Comprehension

All units include a set of reading comprehension questions to check that students understand key points of the unit's reading passage.

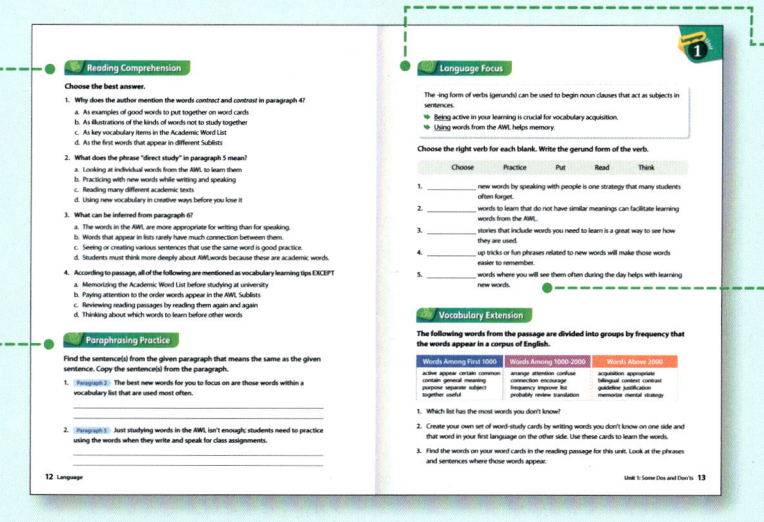

Language Focus

A grammatical structure used in the passage is highlighted for students to review. A short exercise provides additional practice with the target structure.

Vocabulary Extension

A variety of vocabulary development activities across the series help students practice a range of strategies for learning of and about new words.

Paraphrasing Practice

Two paraphrases based on sentences that appear in the reading passage model re-wording techniques students can utilize in their own academic writing.

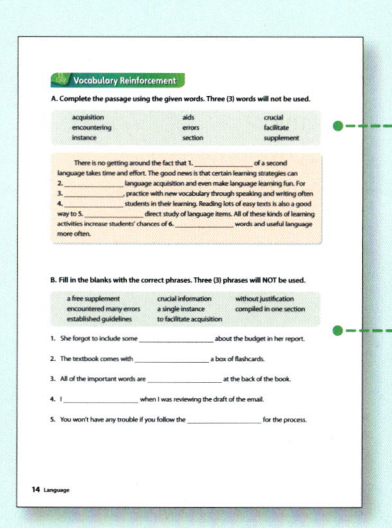

Vocabulary Reinforcement: A

The unit's target words are reviewed in a new context within a paragraph written on a topic related to the unit's reading passage.

Vocabulary Reinforcement: B

The last activity in each unit examines how some of the unit's target words commonly appear in collocations.

Unit 1 Language: Some Dos and Don'ts

Pre-reading Questions

Think about the following questions.

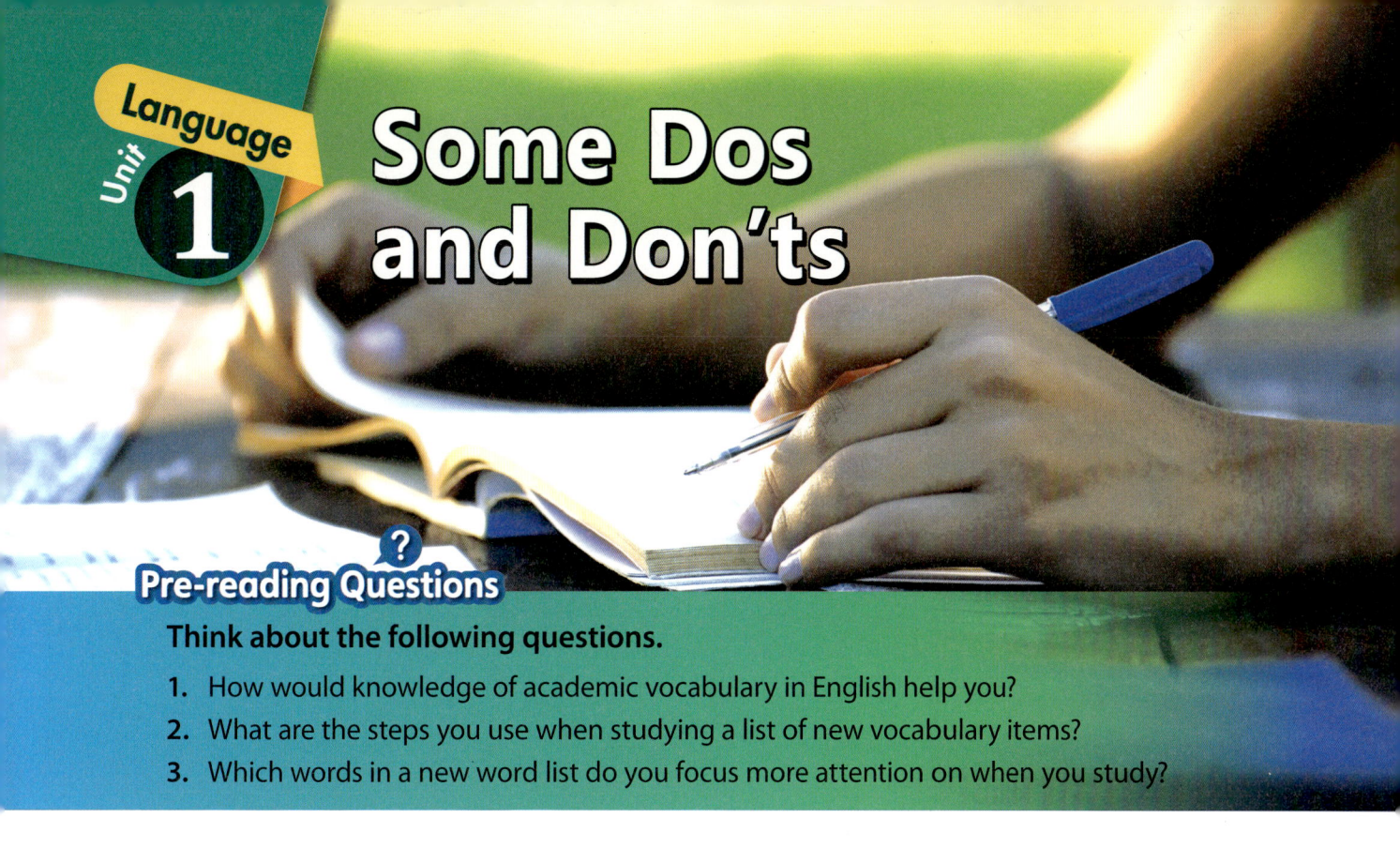

1. How would knowledge of academic vocabulary in English help you?
2. What are the steps you use when studying a list of new vocabulary items?
3. Which words in a new word list do you focus more attention on when you study?

Vocabulary Preview

Write the word that matches the definition.

acquisition	crucial	guideline	instance
justification	section	encounter	error
facilitate	supplement	aid	compiled

1. a mistake — n. _____
2. a situation or event that stands as an example — n. _____
3. one part of a larger whole — n. _____
4. to add other things in order to have a better result — v. _____
5. a useful rule or suggestion within a process — n. _____
6. necessary; critically important — adj. _____
7. to help; to assist — v. _____
8. collected; put together — adj. _____
9. to make a process easier; to act so as to speed up a task — v. _____
10. an understanding that proves why something is true or needed — n. _____
11. to meet; to come into contact with — v. _____
12. the ability or act of getting something; taking something for future use — n. _____

Language

Working with the Academic Word List 🔊 02

🔍 Topic at a Glance

Students face a huge task when they undertake learning another language. For one thing, native speakers of the language know a lot more words than language learners could ever study! However, the task is not impossible. If learners study a small list of important words, they can actually manage well even when studying at a university in their second language. That is, in fact, one of the reasons for the existence of the Academic Word List (AWL). And when it comes to studying the AWL, certain methods can prove more useful for learners than methods they may have used before.

It is important to know what the purpose of a word list is (see Unit 2 of *Reading for the Academic World 1* about the AWL) and how it was made. It is also important to think about how we learn vocabulary and how we can use word lists to help us with this learning. Here are some key points about learning words using the AWL.

5 Firstly, we need to think about choosing words to learn from the list and why we might choose some words over others. In vocabulary, it is more helpful to learn words which occur the most often first. Because these words have high frequency[1], we **encounter** them often in texts and hear them often. Word families in the AWL are arranged
10 according to frequency, with the most frequent words in Sublist[2] One. So Sublist One is a good place to start with the AWL. If you know all the words in Sublist One, then move on to Sublist Two, and carry on down the list to Sublist Ten, which contains the least frequent word families of the AWL.

You can use the AWL as a checklist for words you find in texts. If you find words from
15 your texts in the AWL, then they are probably useful words for you to learn. Think carefully about words that are not in the AWL. If you don't think they are general high frequency words or they are not subject-specific words which are useful for your studies, then there is little **justification** for spending time on learning such words.

A key learning strategy to think about when learning words from lists is keeping
20 words that look or sound the same separate in your learning. It can be easy to confuse words which look or sound the same. For **instance**, *contract* and *contrast* are very similar words in the AWL—they only differ in one letter and appear next to each other in the list of AWL headwords[3]. This means these two words can be difficult to learn if you learn them together. Another useful learning **guideline** is to avoid words that all start with the

---

[1] frequency (n.) — a measure of how often something repeats
[2] sublist (n.) — a list that is under or within a larger list
[3] headword (n.) — an easily recognized word form, to which frequent, regular, transparent affixes may be attached to construct other known forms of the word

same letter or that have similar meanings because they are easily confused too. Choosing words to learn that do not look the same or sound the same or have similar meanings can **facilitate** learning words from the AWL.

Certain **sections** of units within this book have some examples of strategies you can use to study words directly from the AWL, such as word cards. Direct study is a good way to learn words, but it is not the only way. Learners need to read as much as possible and listen as much as possible to meet the words in the AWL in context. Learners also need to write academic texts and talk about academic topics to practice these words. In this textbook[4], texts contain words from the AWL, and tasks encourage you to focus on aspects of the words' meanings and form. This practice is useful, but it needs to be **supplemented** by strategies for learning and extra independent practice like speaking, writing and listening. Using words from the AWL helps memory. There is a saying in English: If you don't use it, you lose it!

One common **error** in using **compiled** lists of vocabulary words is to try to memorize[5] all the words in the list without really paying attention to what they mean or why they are important. Try to think deeply as you are learning more about the words in the AWL (and any other kind of vocabulary too). If you try to make lots of mental connections with words, it can **aid** learning. For instance, think of times you might use words from the AWL in your speaking and writing or try to imagine contexts which might be appropriate for using the words.

And finally, being active in your learning is **crucial** for vocabulary **acquisition**, as much as it is for learning other things. Make time to review your vocabulary regularly, for instance, by rereading texts from this book often and trying to use your memory to recall the meaning of words from the AWL. If you use bilingual[6] translations of words from the lists, then think about strategies for using your memory, such as covering up one of the words and trying to remember it in the other language without looking. This book has other good strategies and techniques for learning vocabulary. Make sure you read them and think about how you could use some of these ideas for improving your vocabulary learning.

[4] textbook (n.) — a book that is used in some kind of academic class
[5] memorize (v.) — to study something so as to fix that thing in one's mind or memory
[6] bilingual (adj.) — of two languages

Reading Comprehension

Choose the best answer.

1. Why does the author mention the words "contract" and "contrast" in paragraph 4?
    a. As examples of good words to put together on word cards
    b. As illustrations of the kinds of words not to study together
    c. As key vocabulary items in the Academic Word List
    d. As the first words that appear in different Sublists

2. What does the phrase "direct study" in paragraph 5 mean?
    a. Looking at individual words from the AWL to learn them
    b. Practicing with new words while writing and speaking
    c. Reading many different academic texts
    d. Using new vocabulary in creative ways before you lose it

3. What can be inferred from paragraph 6?
    a. The words in the AWL are more appropriate for writing than for speaking.
    b. Words that appear in lists rarely have much connection between them.
    c. Seeing or creating various sentences that use the same word is good practice.
    d. Students must think more deeply about AWL words because these are academic words.

4. According to the passage, all of the following are mentioned as vocabulary learning tips EXCEPT
    a. Memorize the Academic Word List before studying at university.
    b. Pay attention to the order words appear in the AWL Sublists.
    c. Review reading passages by reading them again and again.
    d. Think about which words to learn before other words.

Paraphrasing Practice

Find the sentence(s) from the given paragraph that means the same as the given sentence. Copy the sentence(s) from the paragraph.

1. **Paragraph 2** The best new words for you to focus on are those words within a vocabulary list that are used most often.

   _____
   _____

2. **Paragraph 5** Just studying words in the AWL isn't enough; students need to practice using the words when they write and speak for class assignments.

   _____
   _____

Language Focus

> The *-ing* form of verbs (gerunds) can be used to begin noun clauses that act as subjects in sentences.
>
> ➥ <u>Being</u> active in your learning is crucial for vocabulary acquisition.
> ➥ <u>Using</u> words from the AWL helps memory.

Choose the right verb for each blank. Write the gerund form of the verb.

Choose	Practice	Put	Read	Think

1. _____ new words by speaking with people is one strategy that many students often forget.

2. _____ words to learn that do not have similar meanings can facilitate learning words from the AWL.

3. _____ stories that include words you need to learn is a great way to see how they are used.

4. _____ up tricks or fun phrases related to new words will make those words easier to remember.

5. _____ words where you will see them often during the day helps with learning new words.

Vocabulary Extension

The following words from the passage are divided into groups by frequency that the words appear in a corpus of English.

Words Among First 1,000	Words Among 1,000-2,000	Words Above 2,000
active appear certain common contain general meaning purpose separate subject together useful	arrange attention confuse connection encourage frequency improve list probably review translation	acquisition appropriate bilingual context contrast guideline justification memorize mental strategy

1. Which list has the most words you don't know?

2. Create your own set of word study cards by writing words you don't know on one side and the words in your first language on the other side. Use these cards to learn the words.

3. Find the words on your word cards in the reading passage for this unit. Look at the phrases and sentences where those words appear.

Vocabulary Reinforcement

A. Complete the passage using the given words. Three words will NOT be used.

acquisition	aids	crucial
encountering	errors	facilitate
instance	section	supplement

There is no getting around the fact that 1. _____ of a second language takes time and effort. The good news is that certain learning strategies can 2. _____ language acquisition and even make language learning fun. For 3. _____, practice with new vocabulary through speaking and writing often 4. _____ students in their learning. Reading lots of easy texts is also a good way to 5. _____ direct study of language items. All of these kinds of learning activities increase students' chances of 6. _____ words and useful language items more often.

B. Fill in the blanks with the correct phrases. Three phrases will NOT be used.

a free supplement	crucial information	without justification
encountered many errors	a single instance	compiled in one section
established guidelines	to facilitate acquisition	

1. She forgot to include some _____ about the budget in her report.

2. The textbook comes with _____—a box of flashcards.

3. All of the important words are _____ at the back of the book.

4. I _____ when I was reviewing the draft of the email.

5. You won't have any trouble if you follow the _____ for the process.

14 Language

Unit 2 Language: Choosing Your Words

Innovations

Pre-reading Questions

Think about the following questions.

1. What are the most frequent words in your first language?
2. Are they short words or long words?
3. Which of these two words is worth learning first—*help* or *assist*? Why?

Vocabulary Preview

Write the word that matches the definition.

assign	comprise	enable	estimate
paragraph	integral	proportion	site
access	investment	portion	priority

1. a place; a page on the internet — n. _____
2. the time, money, or effort put into doing something — n. _____
3. a section; a small number out of a whole amount — n. _____
4. to make possible; to give some ability — v. _____
5. a share; a percentage — n. _____
6. the order of importance given to several things — n. _____
7. to make up or form; to include — v. _____
8. necessary; essential — adj. _____
9. several sentences that appear together related to a topic — n. _____
10. to use facts to guess a number or amount — v. _____
11. the ability or right to use or enter — n. _____
12. to give work to another; to say what task must be done by someone — v. _____

Language

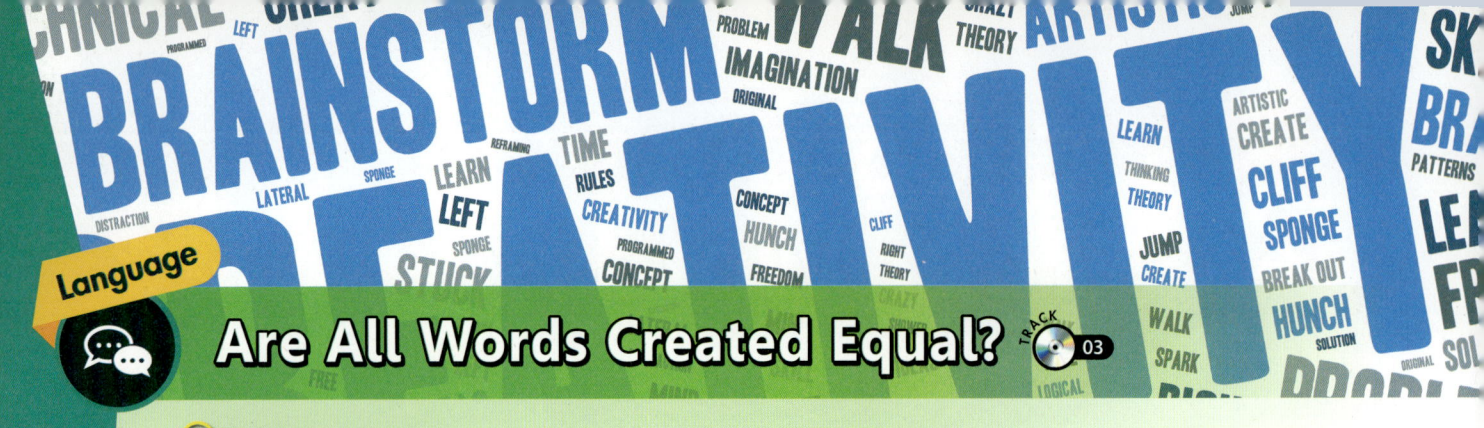

Are All Words Created Equal? TRACK 03

🔍 Topic at a Glance

A high frequency word is one that readers see regularly while reading. There are actually a small number of common words that make up the majority of any English text. With the help of the internet, students of English can easily find many high frequency word lists to study. However, students will find that high frequency word lists from different sources are not all the same. The good news is that most lists share a lot of the same words among the first 300 words. Readers who are able to read high frequency words quickly and understand them easily are well on their way to becoming fluent readers in English.

A rather small number of words are very frequent.

The ten most frequent words in English typically cover 25 percent of the words in any text, and the hundred most frequent words cover around 50 percent. These include words such as *the*, *of*, *be*, and *it*. Have a look at a page and see how often the word *the* occurs. (It
5   occurs in almost every line in this **paragraph**!). By itself, the word *the* covers 7 percent of any written English text. The most frequent thousand words cover around 80 percent of the words in most texts. In some languages, the coverage[1] figures
10 are even higher than this. This means that a rather small group of words make up a large **proportion** of any text.

When learning words, it is good to learn these high frequency words first. The effort of learning these words is well repaid[2] by opportunities to meet and use these words.
15 Vocabulary specialists typically see the high frequency words of English as consisting of around 2,000 to 3,000 words. Only a small **portion** of these words are function words (words like *the*, *a*, *of*, *because*, *it*, *one*, *which*, and *that*). Most are nouns, verbs, adjectives, and adverbs (content words).

If you want to find lists of the most useful words, go to Paul Nation's internet **site** and
20 look at the headwords of the first 10,000 words. These are in groups of one thousand words.

A large number of words are very infrequent.

Half of the words in any text will occur only once in that text. So, if you read a novel which is 100,000 words long from beginning to end, you can **estimate** that it has around 5,000 different words in it. For example, the novel *Captain Blood* is 115,879 words long and
25 is **comprised** of 5,071 different word families. A large number of the different words that

---

[1] coverage (n.) — the extent or degree to which the amount is included
[2] repay (v.) — to return or give back an equal amount

16 Language

you meet in that novel (well over 2,000) will occur only once. That means there will not be repeated opportunities to encounter these words in the novel to help learn them, and if you look them up in a dictionary and study them, you may have to wait a long time before you encounter them anywhere else again. All books are like this. They are comprised of many words that are not repeated.

Apply these ideas about words to your learning.

One of the **integral** skills in learning a language is to know what words are worth learning at each stage of your proficiency[3] development. First, you should find out how many words you know. You can do this easily at www.myvocabularysize.com. If you know 2,000 words, then the third 1,000 words should be your next **priority** level to learn. You can find a list of these words on Paul Nation's website under the heading *Headwords of the first 10,000 words*. You can then choose graded readers at that word level.

Because there are many low frequency words, it is best to read material that uses a controlled vocabulary so that your time is not spent on low frequency words that are not useful for you at your present level of proficiency. Graded readers written with controlled vocabulary are excellent materials for this kind of language practice. Almost every word you meet in a graded reader is worth learning, and so you should put them on word cards or in flash card programs to learn them.

If you are **assigned** a difficult book to read that contains many unfamiliar words, you need to be strategic about your vocabulary learning so that you don't waste time on words that are not useful for you at present. If possible, read the book electronically with an e-reader device so that you have **access** to the definitions of words easily. On many e-reader devices, the meaning is provided above words that you tap. Don't learn every new word you meet. It is not worth the **investment** of your study time. Only learn those that are in the next 1,000 words you need to learn or are very closely related to the content of what you are reading.

Reread the book within a month or two of having read it the first time. It should be much easier this time and the repetition will help with vocabulary acquisition. This kind of practice will also **enable** you to deepen[4] your understanding of what you have read.

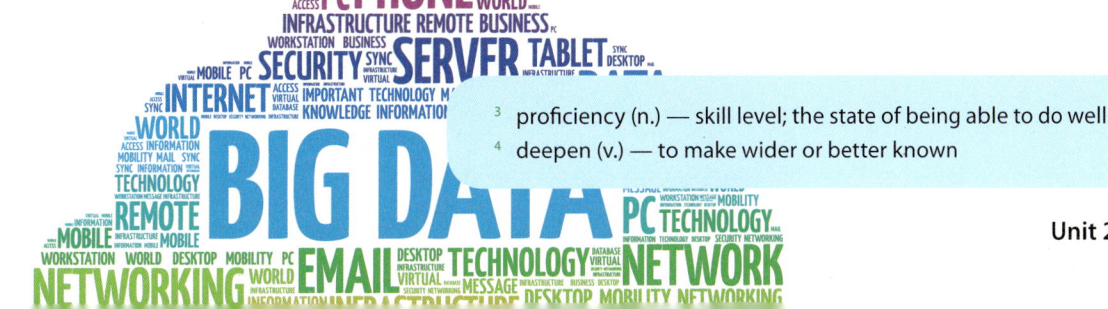

---

[3] proficiency (n.) — skill level; the state of being able to do well
[4] deepen (v.) — to make wider or better known

Reading Comprehension

Choose the best answer.

1. **All of the following are true about high frequency words EXCEPT**
   a. High frequency words cover a large proportion of a text.
   b. There are around 10,000 high frequency words.
   c. High frequency words include function words.
   d. High frequency words should be learned first.

2. **Around half of the different words in a novel are**
   a. specific to the novel's subject and rarely worth learning.
   b. low frequency words that are seldom used by speakers today.
   c. not repeated after they appear the first time in the story.
   d. frequently repeated in the same context, but not very often in new contexts.

3. **It is easier to choose what books to read if you know**
   a. your vocabulary size.
   b. the function words of English.
   c. what words are not repeated.
   d. whether the book contains high frequency words.

4. **What is a good guideline for readers to follow?**
   a. Put all the unknown words you meet onto word cards.
   b. Don't waste time rereading books you have read before.
   c. Learn around 1,000 words before you try to read a book.
   d. While reading, carefully choose which words to learn.

Paraphrasing Practice

Find the sentence(s) from the indicated paragraph that means the same as the given sentence. Copy the sentence(s) from the paragraph.

1. Paragraph 5 As students' levels of English change, it is important for them to figure out which words are most useful for them to study next.

   _____
   _____

2. Paragraph 7 It is a waste of time and effort for students to try and learn every word they don't know when they're reading.

   _____
   _____

Language Unit 2

Language Focus

> Use either *to* or *so that* to express purpose. Follow *to* with a phrase. Follow *so that* with a clause.
>
> ➨ Put the words from a graded reader on word cards <u>to</u> learn them.
> ➨ You need to be strategic about your vocabulary learning <u>so that</u> you don't waste time on words that are not useful for you.

Write *to* or *so that* to complete each sentence.

1. Aim to learn about 25 new words per week _____ keep your learning goals realistic and achievable.

2. Read books electronically with an e-reader device _____ you have access to the definitions of words easily.

3. It is best to read material that uses a controlled vocabulary _____ your time is not spent on low frequency words.

4. Picture something in your mind and relate it to a word _____ it is easier to remember the word.

5. Reread books a month or two later _____ deepen your understanding of what you have read.

Vocabulary Extension

Write the words below with the same suffixes together as a group. What do you think is the function of each suffix? Check the function in the appendix.

acquisition	advantage	coverage	delivery	finalist	inquiry
motivation	proficiency	proportion	specialist	typist	usage

Group 1	Group 2	Group 3	Group 4

suffix 1: _____ suffix 2: _____ suffix 3: _____ suffix 4: _____

function: _____ function: _____ function: _____ function: _____

Unit 2: Choosing Your Words

Vocabulary Reinforcement

A. Complete the passage using the given words. Three words will NOT be used.

assign	investment	portion
comprised	enable	estimate
integral	site	access

With advances in hand-held technology, tablets and e-readers are becoming 1. _____ parts of many language programs. In some cases, teachers 2. _____ a single book for the whole class to read. In other classrooms, students are given 3. _____ to online libraries through their electronic devices. Such libraries 4. _____ students of different levels to choose books individually to read. These online libraries may be 5. _____ of both graded readers as well as regular books. The initial 6. _____ in electronic devices and online libraries may seem large, but many programs are finding it well worth the cost.

B. Fill in the blanks with the correct phrases. Three phrases will NOT be used.

a good investment	cut into portions	enables full access
an integral part	assigned work	comprise a paragraph
estimate the proportion	set priorities	

1. A topic and supporting ideas are the key parts that _____.

2. From the data, we can _____ of shoppers in the store who are male.

3. Sharing ideas with others is _____ of each lesson in our English class.

4. Some people don't know how to _____ in their lives.

5. The correct user ID and password _____ to the internet site.

Unit 3 History: Inventors Who Changed Our Lives

Pre-reading Questions

Think about the following questions.

1. Which invention is the most important in the world?
2. Who are the most famous inventors you know?
3. What is something that needs to be invented?

Vocabulary Preview

Write the word that matches the definition.

revolutionize	compensation	label	appreciate
credit	equipment	ensure	contribute
element	discrimination	demonstrate	chemical

1. to change something completely — v. _____
2. a payment for doing a job — n. _____
3. a word or phrase that describes someone — n. _____
4. to make certain something is safe — v. _____
5. to understand the importance of something or someone — v. _____
6. a basic substance made up of atoms of only one kind — n. _____
7. the supplies or tools needed for a special purpose — n. _____
8. to help cause something to happen — v. _____
9. a substance used in or resulting from a process in chemistry — n. _____
10. to show or explain how something is used or done — v. _____
11. the special praise or attention given to someone for doing something important — n. _____
12. the practice of unfairly treating people from a group differently than other people — n. _____

History

Female Inventors: Ahead of Their Times 04

Topic at a Glance

Many people know of Karl Benz, who invented the first car. They also know that the Wright brothers invented the first successful airplane. Some may even know about Benjamin Franklin, who invented bifocal glasses. However, many women have also contributed to science throughout the years, though they have not been given credit in science and history books. This is a shame because we use many of their inventions in our daily lives. Some contributions changed our lives a great deal. Others simply made all of our lives a little bit easier.

The word "genius" is thrown around quite a bit. Many people have been given the **label**, but few truly live up to it. Women with the label of genius have endured[1] stereotypes and **discrimination**. However, they have played an important role in leading the way toward inventions and discoveries that have changed our lives. Their inventions have made
5 life easier for people all over the world. Other women have **revolutionized** science and math in ways that are only just now being understood.

Some inventions that have made life easier are the dishwasher and the ice cream maker. In 1843, Nancy Johnson created a machine that was an immediate hit with kids everywhere. She invented a hand-operated ice cream maker.
10 The inner bowl included a turning paddle[2] to mix the ingredients. The outer bowl held salt and ice, which helped freeze the ice cream while allowing the person turning the handle to mix it. Both children and adults **appreciated** this easy way of making such a delicious dessert. Josephine Cochrane invented the first dishwashing machine in 1886. She was tired of her servants chipping her expensive china dishes. She measured all of the dishes
15 and made wire compartments[3] to place them in. Her invention was the first to use water pressure to shoot hot, soapy water onto the dishes inside the machine.

Other inventions have the practical application of making life safer. Mary Anderson invented the first hand-operated wiper for car windows in 1903. It required users to use their hand to pull a lever[4] to remove ice and snow from the window. Some did not feel it
20 was safe because drivers had to do two things at once. It did not have commercial success because car companies did not feel that it would be necessary in commercial use. However, when her patent ran out in 1920, a large car company used her design and made it standard **equipment** in all of their cars. She never received any **compensation** for her contribution.

In 1882, Maria Beasley invented the life raft. She was concerned about people's lives

---

[1] endure (v.) — to suffer through; to put up with
[2] paddle (n.) — something with a handle and flat head, used for moving or pushing liquid
[3] compartment (n.) — a small box or space to put things in
[4] lever (n.) — a handle that can be moved up or down to operate a machine

25 while they traveled on the water. She wanted to **ensure** their safety by building something that would not catch on fire, was small, and could be put to sea quickly. Her life raft had metal floats and rails[5] on its sides. It could also be easily and quickly folded for storage. In fact, her invention saved hundreds of lives during the sinking of the *Titanic*.

Another invention used to keep people safe was developed by Stephanie Kwolek in 1965. She began working for a **chemical** company after graduating from college. While working on developing manmade fibers[6], she invented a strong and lightweight fiber that is five times stronger than steel. This later developed into what we now know as Kevlar. It is used in body armor[7], tennis rackets, bike helmets, and work gloves, among other things.

35 Other discoveries led to huge advances in science with lasting effects. Marie Curie is often called the First Lady of Science. She was also the first person to win two Nobel Prizes. In the early 1900s, she developed and coined the term *radioactivity*. Her research led her to discover two entirely new **elements** in chemistry: polonium and
40 radium. This resulted in the development of mobile[8] X-ray machines. Her work revolutionized both chemistry and physics. Sadly, she died as a direct result of her work with the substances she studied.

Anyone in the field of computer science will know Grace Hopper. In 1944, she helped design and build the first computer, which took up an entire room. She later developed the
45 first modern computer language. Many computer scientists believed that computers could only be used to do mathematical calculations. She **demonstrated** that there were many other uses and developed a language that could be used for business.

When you ask most people who discovered DNA's complex shape in the 1960s, they will probably name two men if they know biology well. However, the discovery was first
50 made by biophysicist Rosalind Franklin in 1953. She was the first to capture evidence of the shape of DNA in a photograph. Her research was stolen, and she was not given **credit** until years later.

There are many inventions and discoveries that have been made throughout the years. It is important to give women credit for what they have achieved where it is due. Too
55 often, the things they **contributed** to science have not been properly appreciated. Either their inventions or discoveries were not taken seriously in their time or their contributions were only recognized years later. Thankfully, they held to their belief in science and ignored or fought discrimination in their path.

[5] rail (n.) — a metal guard to keep one from falling off the edge of something
[6] fiber (n.) — a single long, thin string
[7] armor (n.) — a strong suit, usually of metal, worn to protect one's body
[8] mobile (adj.) — able to be moved or carried

Reading Comprehension

Choose the best answer.

1. Which of the following is true according to paragraph 3?
   a. Anderson listed her patent in 1920.
   b. Anderson invented the first automatic windshield wiper.
   c. A car company used Anderson's design in their cars after her patent expired.
   d. Anderson was compensated greatly by the car company who used her design.

2. What can be inferred about Kwolek's invention, Kevlar?
   a. Many lives have been saved by it.
   b. Nothing is stronger than steel.
   c. Kevlar has limited uses.
   d. Natural fibers would be stronger than Kevlar.

3. Which of the following is NOT true about Marie Curie?
   a. She was the first woman to win two Nobel Prize Awards.
   b. She made two new discoveries in biology.
   c. She died because of her research.
   d. She helped revolutionize science as we know it.

4. According to paragraph 7, which of the following best describes Grace Hopper?
   a. She invented a computer language that only used mathematics.
   b. She helped build what is now the world's smallest computer.
   c. She proved that computers were best used for calculations.
   d. She helped develop a computer language for a new purpose.

Paraphrasing Practice

Find the sentence(s) from the given paragraph that means the same as the given sentence. Copy the sentence(s) from the paragraph.

1. **Paragraph 6** Marie Curie, the First Lady of Science, won two Nobel Prizes.

   _____
   _____

2. **Paragraph 8** Although Rosalind Franklin's discovery about DNA was used by others who became famous, she was eventually given credit for her work.

   _____
   _____

Language Focus

Conjunctions such as *and*, *or*, and *but* connect words, phrases, or clauses. *And* adds information. *But* shows contrast. *Or* is used to show different options.

- Hopper demonstrated that there were many other uses <u>and</u> developed a language that could be used for business.
- Beasley invented the life raft that was used on the *Titanic*, <u>but</u> few people know this.
- Car wipers are useful to clear water <u>or</u> snow from the car's front window.

Choose the word to complete the sentence.

1. Many people have been given the label genius, (and / but / or) few truly live up to it.

2. The inventions of women were often not taken seriously, (and / but / or) their contributions were only recognized years later.

3. A car company used Anderson's design (and / but / or) made it standard equipment in all of their cars.

4. Cochrane measured all of the dishes (and / but / or) made wire compartments to place them in.

5. Women who worked in science ignored (and / but / or) fought discrimination in their path.

Vocabulary Extension

Hint: A common ending for verb word forms is *-ate*.

Complete the chart.

Noun	Verb	Adjective	Adverb
appreciation	1.	appreciative	appreciatively
2.	equip	equipped	—
chemical	—	3.	chemically
demonstration	4.	demonstrative	demonstratively
compensation	5.	compensatory	—
6.	revolt	revolutionary	—

Unit 3: Inventors Who Changed Our Lives

Vocabulary Reinforcement

A. Complete the passage using the given words. Three words will NOT be used.

compensation	labeled	appreciated
equipment	contribute	element
discrimination	demonstrate	chemical

In the field of science or business, there are individuals who can be
1. _____ "rising stars." These individuals may 2. _____ more in their present position, or they may 3. _____ skills that will lead to future success. A problem, though, is that such individuals often know their worth. They may choose to leave a company or research position where they don't feel
4. _____. They may also ask for higher 5. _____ for their work from managers or heads of research. Co-workers or fellow researchers who see different treatment of these stars may not like such 6. _____. This may lead to division in a work or research team.

B. Fill in the blanks with the correct phrases. Three phrases will NOT be used.

given credit	chemical elements	standard equipment
ignore discrimination	revolutionized science	chemical company
things they contribute	ensure the safety	

1. Lifeboats are now _____ in all ships.

2. Some female scientists were never _____ for their work until much later.

3. There have been many discoveries throughout the years that have _____.

4. It seems impossible that people could _____ that was so obvious.

5. Airbags are required in cars to _____ of passengers.

26 History

Unit 4 History: Protected by Nature

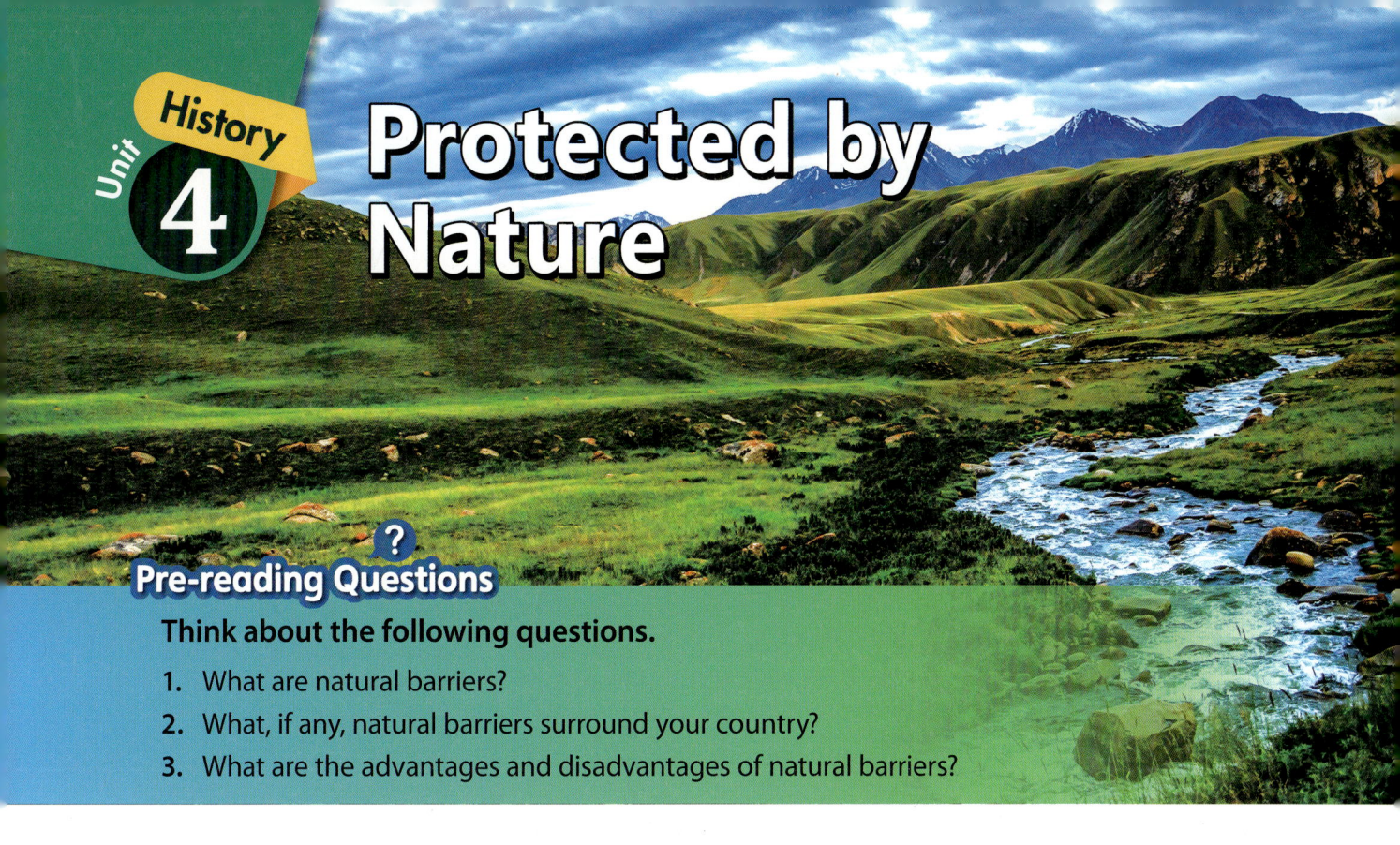

Pre-reading Questions

Think about the following questions.

1. What are natural barriers?
2. What, if any, natural barriers surround your country?
3. What are the advantages and disadvantages of natural barriers?

Vocabulary Preview

Write the word that matches the definition.

channel	commodity	contact	export
exposure	ideology	link	network
resources	route	transport	virtually

1. experience of something — n. _____
2. a group or system of interconnected people or things — n. _____
3. nearly; almost — adv. _____
4. a substance or product that can be traded — n. _____
5. to sell goods or services to another country — v. _____
6. available materials and supplies — n. _____
7. a means or a medium — n. _____
8. a way of conveying people or goods from place to place — n. _____
9. a system of ideas, especially in economic or political policy — n. _____
10. a meeting or relationship — n. _____
11. to connect — v. _____
12. a way or path — n. _____

History

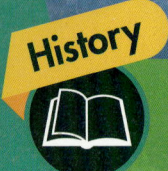

China's Natural Barriers

🔍 Topic at a Glance

Chinese civilization and history can be traced back to around 2000 BC. That is more than 4,000 years! In comparison, the Roman Empire (considered to be one of the greatest civilizations) just lasted 1,200 years from its foundation to its fall. The history of the US as an independent country only spans about 300 years. These numbers speak to how enduring Chinese civilization has been. It is an incredible feat to say the least, and credit is partially due to the country's natural barriers.

Located in Eastern Asia, China is a land measuring more than nine million square kilometers in area today. Ancient China was actually much larger. Enclosed[1] by natural geographical features and bodies of water, China was a difficult land for people to access or for invaders[2] to attack during its ancient days. In fact, for much of its early history, the
5 ancient Chinese believed that they were alone in the world simply for the reason that they did not encounter many other civilizations[3] often.

What are these natural features that protected China from invaders and the rest of the world for such a long time? First, to the north of China were the Gobi and Taklamakan Deserts. The Gobi Desert, which stretches 1,200 kilometers between China
10 and Mongolia, is considered to be the driest desert with less than 200 millimeters of rain per year. In addition, the temperatures vary from −40 °C in the winter to 50 °C in the summer. The Taklamakan Desert in northwest China stretches 1,000 kilometers. It is often referred to as the "Sea of Death" because it has little water, dangerous sandstorms, and poisonous snakes. In addition to its deserts, a land feature protecting China to the south

15 is the Himalayan mountain range, stretching 2,400 kilometers. Not only does the Himalayan mountain range include Mount Everest, the highest peak[4] in the world, but the range also includes nine more of the tallest mountain peaks in the world. The Himalayan
20 mountain range is very difficult not only to climb, but also to pass through. In fact, the mountains **virtually** form a wall to the south of China. Along with deserts

---

[1] enclose (v.) — to be around all sides of something; to surround something
[2] invader (n.) — a person or people who enter a country to take control of it by force
[3] civilization (n.) — an advanced state of culture, science, government, etc. of any society
[4] peak (n.) — the top of a mountain

in the north and mountains in the south, China is surrounded by water on the east—namely, the Yellow Sea, China Sea, and Pacific Ocean. Those who wanted to access China from the east would only be able to do so by ship, which would have been impossible during ancient times as the seas and oceans were too wide and difficult to cross.

Isolated as it was from other civilizations, China developed virtually independent of the rest of the ancient world. Besides the Mongols who lived in the deserts to the north (and only began their threats to invade China in 1000 AD), the ancient Chinese had little knowledge of the other ancient civilizations that existed beyond their borders, such as the ancient Greeks or the ancient Romans or the ancient Egyptians. In fact, they had no knowledge of the ancient Indus Valley Civilization that existed around the same time even though they were only separated by the Himalayan mountain range. Therefore, the ancient Chinese were free to develop and expand with a sense of security and little fear of outside invaders. Another advantage of this isolation[5] is that it also helped to protect the Chinese language, culture, **ideology**, and religion from influence by outside **contact**. However, there were also clear disadvantages to this isolation as well. For example, with no knowledge of other civilizations, there was no ability for the exchange of information or ideas. While this protected their own culture and beliefs, it also limited their **exposure** to other views of the world. In addition, there was no opportunity for the exchange of goods. They had to be self-sufficient and rely only on the inventions of their own people and the **resources** of the land.

It was not until about 200 BC that the ancient Chinese became aware of their neighbors and other civilizations. This knowledge led to the development of the Silk Road, which became a **channel** for **transport** and trade. It was a vast[6] **network** of **routes** that stretched 4,000 kilometers and connected Asia to Europe. These routes were first used during the second century BC and remained important channels of trade for more than 1,500 years. The merchants would travel in caravans[7] and use camels for transport. Cities along the route of the Silk Road were used as stops for rest and water. Through the Silk Road, the Chinese were able to **export** silk, salt, spices, and other goods in exchange for **commodities** such as cotton, ivory, silver, and gold. More importantly, the Silk Road **linked** China to the outside world and allowed for the trade of ideas, culture, and inventions.

The natural barriers[8] of the land served their purpose in helping the civilization of ancient China to grow and expand while protecting it from invaders. And today, these barriers serve as interesting sites for tourists to explore when they visit China.

---

[5] isolation (n.) — the state of being separated from all others
[6] vast (adj.) — very wide; huge
[7] caravan (n.) — a group of pack animals, wagons, or carts that travel together
[8] barrier (n.) — anything that stops other things from passing by or through it

Reading Comprehension

Choose the best answer.

1. According to the passage, all of the following were natural barriers EXCEPT
    a. the extremely dry Gobi and Taklamakan deserts
    b. the vast Pacific Ocean
    c. the Himalayan mountains
    d. the tropical rainforests

2. What can be inferred from paragraph 2?
    a. The Gobi Desert was an effective natural barrier.
    b. The Mongols hated living in the desert.
    c. The Chinese didn't care about interacting with other civilizations.
    d. The Chinese tried to expand beyond their natural barriers.

3. Why does the author mention the Silk Road?
    a. To explain how hard it was for merchants to trade in the desert
    b. To show that the Chinese only interacted with other people when it benefitted them
    c. To suggest that people were eventually able to find routes through the barriers
    d. To describe the difference between roads in the ancient world and modern world

4. What does the term "bodies" in paragraph 1 refer to?
    a. The physical structures of people or animals
    b. The main section of cars
    c. The central part of a writing
    d. An object of measurable size

Paraphrasing Practice

Find the sentence(s) from the given paragraph that means the same as the given sentence. Copy the sentence(s) from the paragraph.

1. **Paragraph 3** The ancient Chinese were privileged with safety and opportunities for undisturbed growth as a people and culture.

_____

_____

2. **Paragraph 4** After 200 BC, goods and ideas were exchanged via the Silk Road.

_____

_____

30 History

Unit 4 History

Language Focus

A series is often written with a conjunction only between the last two items in the list. For variation to add emphasis to the meaning of the sentence, a series can also be written with multiple conjunctions without commas.

A and B and C   A or B or C

➤ The Chinese had little knowledge of ancient civilizations that existed beyond their borders such as the ancient Greeks or the ancient Romans or the ancient Egyptians.

Using the information from the text, fill in the blanks with the most appropriate terms.

1. The Gobi Desert is _____ and _____ and _____.

2. The ancient Chinese did not have to worry about _____ or _____ or _____.

3. The Silk Road connected the people of _____ and _____ and _____.

4. The ancient Chinese exported _____ and _____ and _____.

Vocabulary Extension

Read the example sentences and the definitions for the underlined words. Then choose the best core meaning to match the underlined words.

1. a. The farmer uses a wagon to transport the wood. (to take or carry)
   b. The transport system includes buses and trains. (way of moving)
   c. The story transports readers to another world. (to emotionally carry away)

   transport   interest / lift / move

2. a. My mom likes to watch the shopping channel. (communication frequency)
   b. The report didn't go through the proper channel. (path for sending things)
   c. We took a ferry across the English Channel. (wide body of water)

   channel   connection / empty space / long distance

Unit 4: Protected by Nature 31

Vocabulary Reinforcement

A. Complete the passage using the given words. Three words will NOT be used.

exposure	ideology	link
channel	commodities	export
resources	routes	transport

During the 1800s, it was difficult for countries around the Atlantic to **1.** _____ goods to Asia. The shipping **2.** _____ had to go around the southern tip of either Africa or South America. In the late 1880s, the French began work to dig a **3.** _____ 80 kilometers long across Panama in Central America. They failed in their effort to **4.** _____ the Atlantic to the Pacific, but then the US took up the task again in 1904. Rather than digging a channel, the US built a system of dams and locks across Panama, completed in 1914. Thus, ships filled with **5.** _____ from the East or West could more quickly **6.** _____ their goods from the Atlantic to the Pacific or from the Pacific to the Atlantic.

B. Fill in the blanks with the correct phrases. Three phrases will NOT be used.

a channel to link	lack transport	natural resources
networks of contacts	a strange ideology	commodity for export
transportation routes	virtually no exposure	

1. In both India and China, tea is an important _____.

2. It is hard to find anyone today who has had _____ to television.

3. The internet makes it easy for people to share their _____.

4. Which of the available _____ to the beach takes the least time?

5. One of the candidates for president is promoting _____ that I don't agree with.

Unit 5 Science: The Elements of Disguise

Pre-reading Questions

Think about the following questions.

1. What are some animals you know that look like other things in nature?
2. Why do you think they look this way?
3. Which animal do you think is best at camouflage?

Vocabulary Preview

Write the word that matches the definition.

approach	modified	detection	annual
generation	incompatible	despite	trigger
conformity	adaptation	integration	neutral

1. not bright or strong in color — adj. _____
2. a way of doing something — n. _____
3. not able to be used together — adj. _____
4. covering the period of a year — adj. _____
5. a combination of two things to make one — n. _____
6. the act of discovery — n. _____
7. to cause something else to happen — v. _____
8. similarity in appearance — n. _____
9. changed; adapted — adj. _____
10. in spite of; notwithstanding — prep. _____
11. the change an animal or a plant makes to live in a place — n. _____
12. the average time between the birth of parents and the birth of their children — n. _____

Science

Animals That Hide in Plain Sight 🔊 06

🔍 Topic at a Glance

Many animals have good reason to hide. Other animals are on the lookout for something to eat! Those in danger of being eaten are called prey, and if they stand out, they have a good chance of being eaten. Those that use camouflage to hide have the best change of living and reproducing. Some animals hide by blending into the background. Others try to look like something big or dangerous. Different species have developed a number of interesting ways to camouflage themselves.

In nature, there are typically two different types of animals: prey[1] and predators[2]. Predators hunt other animals for food while prey must learn to avoid being eaten. One **adaptation** that many species have used in both cases, hunting or hiding, is to camouflage[3] themselves. Predators use camouflage to sneak up on their potential meals.
5   Other animals are experts at blending[4] into their environment. Some do not even try to hide, but rather try to look like something dangerous. The use of camouflage varies from species to species.

The natural behavior of the animal and the environment play a role in how their camouflage develops over many **generations**. For example, an insect hiding in a tree will
10 develop a different type of camouflage than an animal with fur. Fish that swim in large schools will hide differently than an animal that flies but finds shelter in trees. In addition, animals do not use camouflage in the same way. This is especially true if a type of camouflage is **incompatible** with helping the animal survive. For example, if a predator is color blind, the prey will not need
15 to match the color of its habitat.

The easiest camouflage technique is for animals to simply blend in with their environment by using the background as their model. This technique, known as concealing[5] coloration, is the most effective **approach** to avoid being seen. Some animals that use concealing coloration
20 to blend into the snow in the Arctic are polar bears and the snowshoe hare. However, the snowshoe hare has an advantage during the summer when it grows brown fur to hide it from predators. The **annual** change of the seasons, which includes the amount of light available during the day, **triggers** the production of hormones[6] in some animals that cause

---

[1] prey (n.) — an animal that is hunted by another animal
[2] predator (n.) — an animal that hunts other animals for food
[3] camouflage (v.) — to cover or disguise oneself with things that look like one's surroundings
[4] blend (v.) — to mix; to combine
[5] concealing (adj.) — hiding; disguising
[6] hormone (n.) — a chemical produced by one's body to start or stop processes in the body

34 Science

them to change colors.

Mammals cannot change their colors rapidly; however, some fish and reptiles certainly can. The octopus is well-known for its ability to change both its color and texture[7] quickly when frightened. The cuttlefish is even faster! It can change color within one second and has the most advanced camouflage of any other animal. The most famous color-changing animal is the chameleon. However, **despite** the belief that animals adapt according to their environment, scientists have discovered that they actually change based on differences in mood. Some small sea creatures are able to change the color of their skin with their diet. This allows them to hide within coral reefs without **detection**.

Disruptive[8] coloration is another technique used by animals to hide the outline of their bodies. This type of camouflage is useful for prey animals that live in large groups. They may use spots, stripes, or other patterns to either appear larger or to hide in shadows. Zebras use the **conformity** of stripes to look like one large animal to lions trying to hunt them. Lions are unable to determine who the smallest or weakest member of the herd is as a result of the pattern. Predators, such as leopards, also use **neutral** disruptive coloration to remain well-hidden in their environment. Their spots enable them to hide themselves within the brush and tall grass, which allows them to hunt more effectively.

The use of disguise is very similar to that of concealing coloration. However, the difference is that animals and insects use their shape and texture, rather than color, to blend into their surroundings. Some examples are the stick insect and the Indian leaf butterfly. The **integration** of such insects and parts of the tree is almost perfect. The thorn bug looks like a sharp spike on a plant stem, which protects both it and the plant. The purpose of this type of camouflage is to look like another object in the animal's environment.

Some animals use mimicry[9] to avoid capture or to make themselves appear more dangerous. Harmless animals or insects are made to look like other creatures that are actually predators. The non-poisonous king snake has similar markings and colorings to the poisonous coral snake. Similarly, the hawk moth caterpillar has **modified** markings on its back that look like a snake head to any predator attempting to sneak up on it from behind.

▲ Coral Snake

▲ King Snake

[7] texture (n.) — the features of a surface that makes it feel a certain way to one's touch
[8] disruptive (adj.) — causing separation or division; interrupting what is normal
[9] mimicry (n.) — the act of copying

Reading Comprehension

Choose the best answer.

1. Which of the following is the best kind of animal camouflage?
   a. Mimicry
   b. Disguise
   c. Concealing
   d. Disruptive

2. Which of the following is NOT true about some animals who use camouflage?
   a. Some animals change their skin by eating different foods.
   b. The octopus can only change its color.
   c. Some non-poisonous snakes look like poisonous ones.
   d. The stick insect looks like part of a tree.

3. How does the snow hare hide itself?
   a. It hides in large groups.
   b. It changes its texture.
   c. It eats a different diet.
   d. It changes with the seasons.

4. What does the author imply by mentioning "generations" in paragraph 2?
   a. Animals best at camouflage are able to have babies that are also good at hiding.
   b. All animals eventually develop the same kind of camouflage.
   c. Insects have the only good camouflage.
   d. Stripes are better than spots when it comes to hiding.

Paraphrasing Practice

Find the sentence(s) from the given paragraph that means the same as the given sentence. Copy the sentence(s) from the paragraph.

1. **Paragraph 5** The best defense for prey animals in large groups is disruptive coloration.

   _____
   _____

2. **Paragraph 7** Harmless animals use mimicry to make themselves look like predators.

   _____
   _____

36 Science

Language Focus

When two sentences show opposition or present surprisingly different information, *however* can be used to logically connect them.

➡ The snowshoe hare uses concealing coloration to blend into the snow in the Arctic. However, during the summer it grows brown fur to hide it from predators.

Choose which of the sentence pairs are correctly linked using *however*.

1. a. Predators hunt prey for food. However, prey can use camouflage to hide themselves.

   b. The natural behavior of the animal plays an important role in how their camouflage develops. However, the camouflage is important.

2. a. Disruptive coloration is a technique used by animals to hide the outline of their bodies. However, they may use spots, stripes, or patterns to hide in the shadows.

   b. Some animals use mimicry to make themselves appear more dangerous. However, they are actually harmless.

Vocabulary Extension

Review the vocabulary word card exercise of practicing words in two languages. Study words going from English to your first language and then from your first language to English.

Work with a partner. Choose any five words from the reading passage. Write the English words here. Can your partner tell you the words in his or her first language?

_____   _____   _____   _____   _____

Work with a partner who knows your first language. Choose any five words from the reading passage that you can translate into your language. Write the words in your language here. Can your partner tell you the words in English?

_____   _____   _____   _____   _____

Study Tip

Don't keep learning the words in the same order.
Keep changing the order of the words in your pack.

Unit 5: The Elements of Disguise

Vocabulary Reinforcement

A. Complete the passage using the given words. Three words will NOT be used.

neutral	modified	detection
generation	incompatible	despite
conformity	adaptation	integration

The kiwi bird of New Zealand lacks **1.** _____ with the image we have of most birds in many ways. **2.** _____ the loss of its ability to fly, the **3.** _____ color of this bird's feathers allows it to camouflage itself near the forest floor. In this way, it escapes **4.** _____ by animals that might want to eat it. Another interesting **5.** _____ of kiwis is their noses. This is the only bird with holes for its nose at the end of its beak. With its **6.** _____ beak, the kiwi can put its beak into the ground and smell insects to eat.

B. Fill in the blanks with the correct phrases. Three phrases will NOT be used.

annual change	incompatible with	most effective approach
many generations	modified markings	neutral coloration
without detection	despite the belief	

1. The leopard was able to hunt the sheep _____ because its spots helped it hide in the tall grass.

2. Some moths have bright _____ that help them look like a larger animal.

3. Concealing coloration is the _____ to avoid being seen.

4. Some chameleons change based on their mood, _____ that they change to hide from predators.

5. Methods of animal camouflage change over the course of _____.

Unit 6 Science: Lights in the Sky

Pre-reading Questions

Think about the following questions.

1. How well are you able to see the sky at night?
2. What do you know about sunspots?
3. What do you know about the aurora borealis?

Vocabulary Preview

Write the word that matches the definition.

fluctuation	attribute	clarity	corresponding
cycle	display	energy	global
nuclear	dynamic	precisely	project

1. involving the entire world — adj. _____
2. an event that impresses or entertains people — n. _____
3. the quality of being easily seen — n. _____
4. relating to using energy that is created when atoms split — adj. _____
5. to send or throw something outward — v. _____
6. a change of level or strength — n. _____
7. active or energetic — adj. _____
8. directly relating to something — adj. _____
9. to say that something is because of something else — v. _____
10. available power — n. _____
11. a set of events that happens on a regular basis — n. _____
12. very accurately — adv. _____

Science: The Auroras

Topic at a Glance

The auroras are well known to people around the world. This beautiful light show in the night sky has been written about in history. Much speculation and mystery have surrounded the auroras. Even cave paintings dating back to before written language existed depict the lights. Philosophers speculated about the meaning of the auroras, while the more superstitious believed they were a sign of imminent death or war. However, Galileo was the first astronomer to actually study and name the lights rather than fear them.

People around the world have known about the aurora borealis for ages. The Romans named the lights after Aurora, the goddess of the morning. This natural light show in the sky is an event that many have traveled thousands of miles to see. The colorful **display** of the lights is **attributed** to charged ions[1] that interact with the earth's magnetic[2] field. Most often known as the northern lights, they can also be seen in the Southern Hemisphere[3], where they are known as the aurora australis.

The dancing lights of the aurora are caused by the yellow sun at the center of our solar system. In a way, our sun acts much like a **nuclear** power plant, having its **energy** stored deep inside. The incredibly hot gases inside of the sun can reach up to 15 million °C at the center. The temperature at the surface, however, is in a constant state of **fluctuation** as the outside of the sun cools and moves about. The magnetic field of the sun twists, creating sunspots on the surface. It took scientists until the 1880s to discover the connection between sunspots and the **corresponding** auroras. When a large cloud of solar particles[4] explodes from the sun, the particles are shot into space and pushed away from the sun at high speeds by the solar wind.

In the 1950s, researchers learned that solar wind was responsible for blowing positive and negative ions toward the earth. It takes about forty hours for the solar wind to **project** the particles to earth. The earth is protected by its magnetic field, which deflects[5] the most powerful particles around or away from our planet. However, the poles have weaker magnetic fields that interact with the sun's ions rather than simply deflecting them. As the

---

[1] ion (n.) — a very small body with a positive or negative charge
[2] magnetic (adj.) — related to the force that can attract things like iron
[3] hemisphere (n.) — a part of a globe or sphere, like the top or bottom or the left or the right
[4] particle (n.) — a very small piece of matter
[5] deflect (v.) — to push away; to turn toward another direction

particles from the sun interact with the earth's magnetic field lines, they release energy to create the remarkable **global** events known as the northern or southern lights. When there are many sunspots on the surface of the sun, auroras can become visible in areas other than the poles.

The different colors seen in the lights are a direct result of the type of gases that are found in the earth's atmosphere. Both the charge on the ions colliding[6] with gases and the altitude[7] at which the particles interact with the magnetic field affect the color. Green aurora is probably the most common color and is produced by oxygen particles about 100 kilometers above the earth. Red auroras are also made from oxygen, but result from collisions at a higher altitude. When collisions occur with nitrogen gas, blue auroras are produced if there is not a lot of oxygen present. Other colors, such as pink, yellow, and violet, are a result of particles colliding with different gases.

What is also interesting is that auroras are visible not only from the earth's surface, but also from space. Pictures of the auroras have been taken by satellites and by the International Space Station. They show up with the most **clarity** when the view of the earth is of the night side of its rotation[8]. The **dynamic** lights of auroras have also been seen in the atmospheres of the outer planets of the solar system, such as Jupiter, Saturn, Uranus, and Neptune.

Solar **cycles** peak every eleven years, with the next peak expected in 2024. Scientists first began keeping records of the cycles of the solar flares in 1749. Since that time, there have been 22 full cycles of storm activity. Though scientists cannot **precisely** predict where solar flares will explode or in which direction, they are able to determine general areas where auroras will be seen. Though they are always present, the best time to see the lights are in winter, on a cold, clear night. The lights are also brighter for two days after many large sunspots are present. Researchers work hard to predict sunspots. The fear is that they have the potential to affect telecommunication systems, satellites, and city power networks. It is hard to imagine that something so beautiful could result from something so disruptive to life as we know it.

---

[6] collide (v.) — to hit with force
[7] altitude (n.) — the distance above the surface of the earth's sea level
[8] rotation (n.) — the act of turning or spinning

Reading Comprehension

Choose the best answer.

1. Which of the following is TRUE?
   a. The auroras are named after a Greek god.
   b. The auroras are caused by charged particles interacting with the moon.
   c. Scientists discovered the connection between sunspots and auroras in the 1880s.
   d. The sun has the same temperature inside and out.

2. What is an important aspect of the magnetic field of the earth?
   a. It protects the earth from most of the sun's solar particles.
   b. It is able to collect the most energetic ions in the solar wind.
   c. It is able to keep solar flares from occurring.
   d. It only lets oxygen particles into the atmosphere.

3. Which of the following is NOT true about the auroras?
   a. Red auroras are made at a higher altitude.
   b. Blue auroras occur when there is a lot of oxygen present.
   c. Green auroras are the most common.
   d. Different colors depend on the types of particles that get hit by ions.

4. What does the term "state" in paragraph 2 mean?
   a. A political region of a country
   b. To say or claim
   c. To list as a fact
   d. A condition in which something exists

Paraphrasing Practice

Find the sentence(s) from the given paragraph that means the same as the given sentence. Copy the sentence(s) from the paragraph.

1. **Paragraph 5** Photos of auroras have been taken by satellites in space.

   _____

   _____

2. **Paragraph 6** The best time to see the lights is on a cold night, two days after large sunspots are present.

   _____

   _____

42 Science

Language Focus

> Compound prepositions are made of two words that act like one-word prepositions. Examples of such prepositions include *away from, inside of, next to, outside of,* etc.
> - The incredibly hot gases <u>inside of</u> the sun can reach up to 15 million °C at the center.
> - The particles are shot into space and pushed <u>away from</u> the sun at high speeds.

Choose the correct compound preposition to complete each sentence.

1. Scientists can't tell (ahead of / next to) time which sunspots will create nice auroras.

2. It takes careful planning (along with / out of) some good luck to schedule a trip during which you hope to view the aurora borealis.

3. Imagine viewing an aurora while sitting (from above / inside of) a plane flying over Canada.

4. (As for / In between) the Aurora Australis, you can only see them if you travel to Antarctica.

5. Find dark places (from among / outside of) areas with cities or streetlights to view auroras.

Vocabulary Extension

Write the words below with the same prefixes together as a group. What do you think each prefix means? Check the meaning in the appendix.

| exit | interview | irrational | explode | irremovable | telecommunication |
| expose | intermediate | irregularly | teleport | international | television |

Group 1	Group 2	Group 3	Group 4

prefix 1: _____   prefix 2: _____   prefix 3: _____   prefix 4: _____

meaning: _____   meaning: _____   meaning: _____   meaning: _____

Vocabulary Reinforcement

A. Complete the passage using the given words. Three words will NOT be used.

display	energy	global
fluctuation	attributed	corresponding
nuclear	precisely	projected

Much like the aurora borealis on Earth, NASA researchers have seen a 1. _____ aurora in the atmosphere of Mars. The 2. _____ of lights in the sky of Mars was recorded at the northern pole of the planet by a NASA satellite. As with the aurora on Earth, the lights on Mars are 3. _____ to particles coming from the Sun. Mars does not have a 4. _____ magnetic field protecting it like Earth. High 5. _____ particles from the Sun are, as a result, 6. _____ deeper into the atmosphere of Mars. The satellite that recorded the aurora on Mars is part of a project begun in 2013 focusing on the study of Mars's atmosphere.

B. Fill in the blanks with the correct phrases. Three phrases will NOT be used.

attributed to	global event	a colorful display
nuclear reactor	more precisely	state of fluctuation
cycles peak	most clarity	

1. Winter is the best time to see the aurora borealis with the _____.

2. Global warming has been _____ many factors.

3. Scientists hope that someday they will be able to predict solar flares _____.

4. Certain male birds will put on _____ to attract a mate.

5. The Sun is always in a _____.

44 Science

Unit 7 Psychology: Make It a Habit!

OLD HABITS → NEW HABITS

Pre-reading Questions

Think about the following questions.

1. What is one of your good habits?
2. What is a habit you would like to change?
3. What kind of habit do you think is difficult for people to change?

Vocabulary Preview

Write the word that matches the definition.

automatic	concentrate	deviation	eliminate
preliminary	hence	journal	minimal
register	resolution	inclination	underlying

1. to record or detect — (v.) _____
2. a change so as to leave or go away from what is normal — (n.) _____
3. as a consequence; therefore — (adv.) _____
4. a daily record of events; a diary — (n.) _____
5. fundamental; basic — (adj.) _____
6. without thought or mental effort — (adj.) _____
7. to remove or get rid of — (v.) _____
8. before others; first — (adj.) _____
9. a fixed decision or promise — (n.) _____
10. of very little amount — (adj.) _____
11. to focus one's attention or mental effort — (v.) _____
12. a comfortable or usual action or thought — (n.) _____

GOOD HABITS

Psychology
The Ins and Outs of Habits

Topic at a Glance

Behavior generally refers to the way in which an individual acts or conducts oneself. It also refers to an individual's manners as well as how a person reacts in a situation. A person can either be aware or unaware of one's behavior. It can also be positive or negative. Everyone has behavioral patterns. However, behavior is not fixed. Actually, behavior is dynamic and changing. People are social beings, which means behavior can be highly dependent on internal and external factors. Some factors might include behavior-based rewards and punishment. Other factors could be the praise or disapproval of others. Still other factors could be internal, such as one's own will or motivations.

Habits, an essential part of life, are a person's **inclination** to follow behaviors or actions that are regularly done. Habits might be associated with a time of day, such as drinking coffee while reading the morning newspaper or watching the evening news daily at 5 p.m. Habits might also relate to the order in which actions are done, such as following
5   a morning routine[1] of brushing one's teeth, taking a shower, getting dressed, and eating breakfast always in that order. Any actions performed with little or no **deviation** from a particular order every day may be considered a habit.

There are good habits and bad habits. Good habits could be related to keeping oneself clean,
10 such as brushing one's teeth, washing one's hands, and showering regularly. Other good habits could be related to a healthy lifestyle, such as taking walks regularly, eating balanced meals, and sleeping and waking early. Following road rules, listening when
15 others are talking, and helping others can also be considered good habits. Of course, there are also bad habits. These might include biting one's nails, waiting until the last night to do one's homework, running late to classes or meetings, and smoking.

How are habits formed? First, a behavior must be learned. When a child learns to
20 walk, it takes time and a lot of energy. The first time a person learns how to drive, it is a slow process that requires one to **concentrate** and use a lot of brain power. It requires thinking, knowing, understanding, and performing each step correctly. After a behavior is learned, the action goes through a habit loop[2], which is a three-step cycle that involves a cue[3], routine, and reward. The **preliminary** cue is a reminder that triggers the thought or behavior. With

---

[1] routine (n.) — a series of actions or steps that are always done in order
[2] loop (n.) — a series of actions or steps that are repeated once a cycle ends
[2] cue (n.) — a word or sign that reminds one to do or say something

46 Psychology

repeated cues, the action becomes a routine. With enough repetition the brain will **register** the action as an **automatic** action. An automatic action that takes **minimal** effort for an adult once learned, such as walking or driving, takes a lot of time and energy for a child to learn initially. This is why habits are important. They **eliminate** the need for our brains to spend energy on creativity or complex thinking in order for our bodies to do certain actions. **Hence**, habits help us manage our minds. In fact, habits make up to 40 percent of our daily actions. Some people call this operating on autopilot. This means we do not think about almost half of the things we do throughout the day. In this way, more of the mind is available for creative or complex activities. Daily habits are important because they are the small activities that make up the ins and outs of the day.

    Habits are not fixed, though. In fact, many people take advantage of the new year to make New Year's **resolutions**, which are promises that people make to themselves or others to improve in a particular area. A person may resolve[4] to change or break a bad habit. Other times, an individual may want to change a habit in order to be more organized or more efficient. Sometimes, a person may want to simply improve oneself or a relationship. The old saying "You can't teach an old dog new tricks" suggests that new habits are difficult to learn—more so as people age. However, it is not impossible and it's never too late. The awareness of the unwanted behavior and the motivation[5] or will to change the habit is the preliminary step to changing a habit. It may help to write down the desired habit in a **journal**. Next, discovering how a habit is formed and identifying the **underlying** cause for the specific habit are important. Then problems should be addressed. It may help to discuss problems and possible solutions with a friend or family member who can check with a person to see if they are keeping on track to break a bad habit.

    Time and repetition are needed to change a habit. Some experts say it takes 28 days to break and make a new habit; others say it can take up to 250 days. In any case, it will take time and patience[6]. In the process of changing a habit, slip-ups may happen. This is not a reason to give up. Instead, write it down, tell the person who is checking if you are on track, and discuss possible reasons for the slip-up and solutions. It's not impossible to learn new tricks!

---

[4] resolve (v.) — to make a promise to oneself
[5] motivation (n.) — the reason one has for doing something
[6] patience (n.) — the ability to wait without complaining or acting to speed things up

Reading Comprehension

Choose the best answer.

1. According to the passage, all of the following are true EXCEPT
    a. Habits take time to break or change.
    b. About 40 percent of our daily actions are habits.
    c. It is impossible for an older person to learn new habits or change old habits.
    d. Keeping a journal or having a partner can help with the process of breaking or changing a habit.

2. What is the correct order of a habit loop?
    a. Routine, reward, cue
    b. Cue, routine, reward
    c. Reward, cue, routine
    d. Routine, cue, reward

3. What does the term "age" in paragraph 4 refer to?
    a. A time in history
    b. Evidence of use over a long time
    c. The time since a person has been born
    d. To become older

4. Why does the author say "Some experts say it takes 28 days to break and make a new habit; others say it can take up to 250 days" in paragraph 5?
    a. To suggest there is no exact science to breaking or making a habit; it varies by individual
    b. To demonstrate how experts do not know much about human habits yet
    c. To support the claim that some habits are easier or harder to make and break
    d. To give a limit of a year for habits to be made or broken

Paraphrasing Practice

Find the sentence(s) from the given paragraph that means the same as the given sentence. Copy the sentence(s) from the paragraph.

1. **Paragraph 3** Learned behaviors are performed through habit loops: cue, routine, and reward.

   _____
   _____

2. **Paragraph 4** Resolutions are decisions to change behaviors for self-improvement.

   _____
   _____

48 Psychology

Language Focus

> An appositive is a noun or pronoun—often with modifiers—set beside another noun or pronoun to explain or identify it. Usually commas appear around the appositive.
>
> ➤ Habits, <u>an essential part of life</u>, are a person's inclination to follow behaviors or actions that are regularly done.

Underline the appositive. Then place commas in the sentences where necessary.

1. Behavior the term for one's actions can be positive or negative.

2. Learning to walk or drive an automatic action that takes minimal effort for adults once learned takes a lot of time and energy for a child to learn initially.

3. Charles Duhigg the man who coined the term habit loop wrote two books on habits and productivity.

4. Awareness the first step to changing one's habit is often the hardest to admit to.

Vocabulary Extension

Hint: A common ending for adjective word forms is *-ing*.

Complete the chart.

Noun	Verb	Adjective	Adverb
inclination	incline	1.	—
registration	register	2.	—
deviation	deviate	3.	undeviatingly
automation	automate	automatic	4.
5.	resolve	resolved	resolvedly
minimum	6.	minimal	minimally

Unit 7: Make It a Habit! **49**

Vocabulary Reinforcement

A. Complete the passage using the given words. Three words will NOT be used.

journal	minimal	preliminary
registers	eliminated	hence
inclination	resolution	underlying

Have you ever made a(n) 1. _____ to try and change yourself to be a happier person? It may be true that we are born with a certain 2. _____ personality or mood; 3. _____, some might say it's impossible to change yourself. But here are some 4. _____ changes you can make in your day, and they just might make you smile more! Keep a(n) 5. _____ of three good things that happen every day. Get out and exercise in the sun. Spend thirty minutes doing something you enjoy. When little things like this become a habit every day, you may develop the 6. _____ to smile a whole lot more.

B. Fill in the blanks with the correct phrases. Three phrases will NOT be used.

small deviation	automatic response	concentrated all his energy
minimal concentration	underlying cycle	journal of resolutions
a preliminary step	recognize the trigger	

1. A delicious result can come from just a _____ from the original recipe.

2. After 40 years behind the wheel, he was able to drive with _____.

3. The family decided to keep a _____ to track their progress.

4. He _____ on completing the project and forgot to eat lunch or dinner.

5. Once the teacher was able to _____ that was causing the child's outbursts, she was able to manage his behavior more effectively.

Unit 8 Psychology: Dancing Until You Drop

Pre-reading Questions

Think about the following questions.

1. How often do you go dancing?
2. What is your favorite kind of dancing?
3. What is the longest you have ever danced?

Vocabulary Preview

Write the word that matches the definition.

abnormally	civil	participate	compound
environmental	exhibit	region	phenomenon
rational	validity	psychological	alternative

1. relating to the mind — adj. _____
2. to take part in an activity or event with others — v. _____
3. to make something worse — v. _____
4. of the conditions that surround or affect someone or something — adj. _____
5. to show or reveal something — v. _____
6. the quality of being real or correct — n. _____
7. a part of a country that is different or distinct in some way — n. _____
8. offering a choice — adj. _____
9. based on facts, not emotions — adj. _____
10. a thing that is interesting or different that can be studied — n. _____
11. unusually; in a way that can cause problems — adv. _____
12. relating to the regular business of a town — adj. _____

Psychology

The Plague of the Dance 09

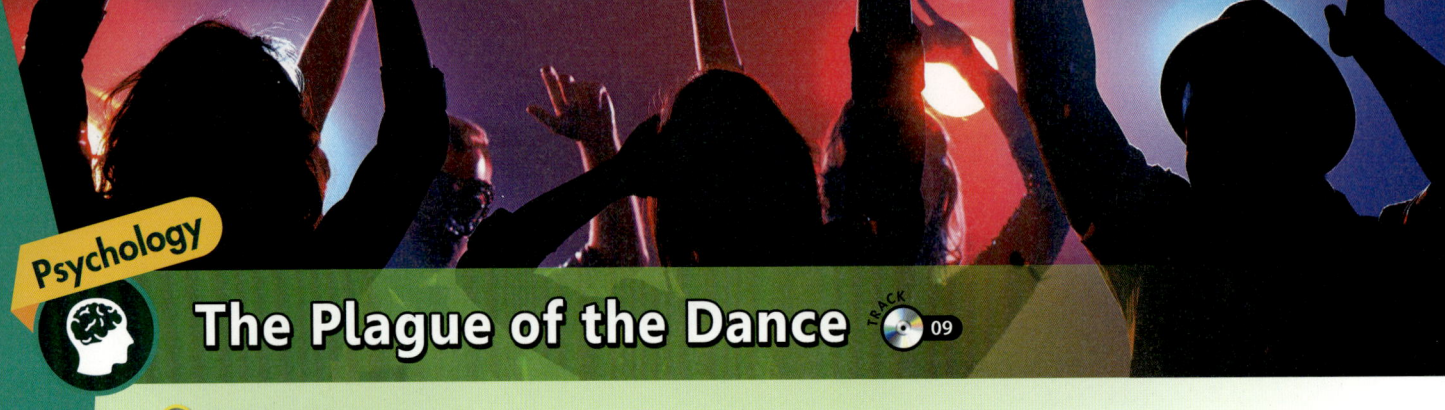

Topic at a Glance

There have been many events throughout history that are unexplained. The Dancing Plague of 1518 is one such event. Over the course of just one month, hundreds of people joined together to dance. People came together and danced nonstop, without any rest, for about a month. Many of them died from exhaustion, heart attacks, and strokes. While historical evidence exists to back this event up, the reason behind it remains unexplained. In fact, of all such dancing events throughout history, none have been so well documented.

Cases of mass hysteria have been recorded throughout history. Mass hysteria happens when people in one group all begin behaving **abnormally**. At times, it comes from an **environmental** factor, such as a fear of contaminated[1] water. Hysteria can develop within a group of people under psychological or emotional stress when pressure that the community is under becomes too much for them to handle. People may **exhibit** physical symptoms[2] that they cannot control. Whatever the reason for its beginning, symptoms of hysteria usually end quickly, and people are left scratching their heads as to what just happened.

The Dancing Plague[3] of 1518 is one of the most confusing events in history. People literally danced themselves to death one summer in Strasbourg, France. The story begins with one woman, Frau Troffea. One morning, she stepped outside and simply started to dance. There was no music or singing, and she exhibited no joy at dancing. In fact, she appeared unable to stop her dancing in any way. It is believed that her constant dancing lasted four to six days. Doctors were called in to diagnose[4] this strange problem. City elders and priests did not simply say it was due to a demon[5] controlling her or because she had lost her reason, as soon neighbor after neighbor began to **participate**. By the end of that first week, at least 34 others had joined her. During that hot month in August, nearly 400 people had joined in the dancing.

Although it may seem strange, the leaders of the town and doctors agreed that the only cure for those with the plague was to

---

[1] contaminated (adj.) — dirty; not pure
[2] symptom (n.) — a sign or condition that indicates a disease or health problem
[3] plague (n.) — a disease that is spread to many people and can end in death
[4] diagnose (v.) — to study the symptoms of sick people and name the diseases they have
[5] demon (n.) — an evil spirit being; a spirit who does bad things that help the Devil

dance even more. They had determined their citizens had "hot blood," and thus dancing was the only cure. They opened up two halls and a market, and even constructed a stage where musicians were able to play for those overcome with the plague. The leaders hired professional dancers to help keep the plague victims on their feet. Many died due to exhaustion and heart attacks. By September, the dancers that remained were taken to a shrine[6] in the **region** to pray for forgiveness, and the plague ended as quickly as it had begun.

There is some doubt as to the **validity** of the dancing plague. However, evidence can be found to show that the event did occur. Historical documents, such as doctors' notes, church sermons[7], and **civil** papers, list dates and details about the event. There have been no widely accepted theories as to why the dancing began, nor any reason as to why it stopped. It is an event of mass hysteria that has puzzled historians for centuries. Some historians have guessed that ergot, a fungus found in wheat and rye, was the cause of the changes in the people of the town. This theory does not have much backing because while ergot may cause spasms[8], it also makes normal movement difficult. Therefore, the people should have been in a trance[9]-like state, unable to move. Another theory is that the dancers were part of a strange religion. This is also unlikely because witnesses have said that the dancers acted as if they wished to stop but were unable to do so. The dancers were also not accused of any wrong belief by the church.

An **alternative** hypothesis as to the cause of the plague relates to the curse of St. Vitus. Perhaps the small town of Strasbourg succumbed to belief in this curse. St. Vitus was the saint of epilepsy[10]. Most Catholics believed he had the power to curse people with a kind of forced dancing if they angered him. The people of the town knew about and feared this curse of St. Vitus. That fear, **compounded** by their other harsh realities, may have resulted in the dancing plague. In addition, the **phenomenon** may have become less and less likely to reoccur over the next few years because belief in saints died out in the region when people changed religions from Catholicism to Protestantism.

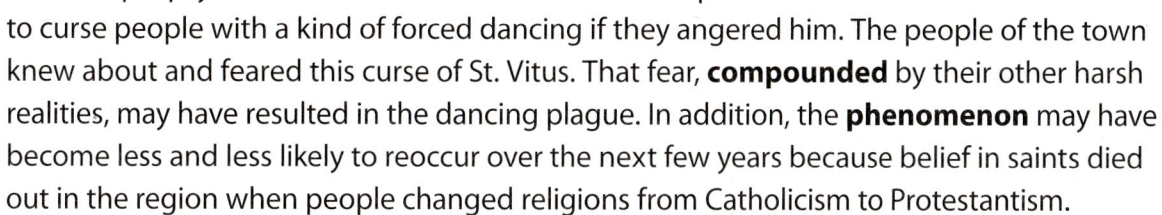

Many historians hold to the belief that this particular case of mass hysteria is a result of extreme **psychological** stress brought on by a lack of food in the region. Though there had been many other smaller dancing plagues, the Dancing Plague of 1518 remains of interest because it was documented so well. Over the next few centuries, religious beliefs in Europe slowly gave way to science and **rational** thinking. This could be the explanation as to why dancing plagues eventually disappeared.

---

[6] shrine (n.) — a holy place, usually where the bones of a saint were buried
[7] sermon (n.) — the message that a priest or pastor delivers during a church service
[8] spasm (n.) — a movement of a person's arms, legs, or other body parts that can't be controlled
[9] trance (n.) — a state in which a person seems to be sleeping but can talk or respond to commands
[10] epilepsy (n.) — a problem with a person's nervous system that causes him or her to lose attention or, in extreme cases, to suffer body spasms and faint

Reading Comprehension

Choose the best answer.

1. All of the following relate to the case of mass hysteria described in the passage EXCEPT
   a. It started when one person began acting abnormally.
   b. It led to a hunt for witches in the region.
   c. It occurred in a small town in Europe.
   d. It lasted for only a few weeks.

2. Why did the author mention "hot blood" in paragraph 3?
   a. Because people were very angry
   b. Because people enjoyed dancing
   c. Because people wanted to build a market
   d. Because the doctors said people had it

3. Which of the following is NOT true about St. Vitus?
   a. He was Catholic.
   b. He was the saint of dancing.
   c. People of the town feared him.
   d. People believed he could curse them with dancing.

4. According to the passage, which of the following is TRUE about the dancing plague?
   a. The dancers were part of a strange religion.
   b. The people of the town ate ergot.
   c. Four hundred people were affected by the dancing plague.
   d. There is no documented evidence that the dancing plague occurred.

Paraphrasing Practice

Find the sentence(s) from the given paragraph that means the same as the given sentence. Copy the sentence(s) from the paragraph.

1. **Paragraph 4** Historians do not think that ergot is the reason the people of the town danced because it makes movement difficult.

   _____
   _____

2. **Paragraph 5** The people of the town probably believed that victims were under the curse of St. Vitus, who cursed people with dancing.

   _____
   _____

54 Psychology

Language Focus

The phrase *as to* can be used to mean *about* or *concerning*.

➡ There have been no widely accepted theories <u>as to</u> why the dancing began, nor any reason <u>as to</u> why it stopped.

Match the parts to make correct sentences.

1. People are left scratching • • as to the validity • • eventually disappeared.
2. There is some doubt • • the cause of the plague relates • • just happened.
3. An alternative hypothesis as to • • as to why dancing plagues • • of the dancing plague.
4. This could be the explanation • • their heads as to what • • to the curse of St. Vitus.

Vocabulary Extension

Read the dictionary definitions below. Find the words in the Vocabulary Preview list on page 51 that match these definitions.

1. _____	*adjective* 1. composed of two or more parts. 2. having or involving two or more actions or functions. *noun* 3. something formed by combining parts. 4. Chemistry. a pure substance made of two or more elements. *verb (used with an object)* 5. to put together into a whole; to combine. 6. to settle or adjust by agreement, especially for a reduced amount, as a debt. 7. to pay (interest) on the accrued interest as well as the principal. 8. to increase or add to. *verb (used without an object)* 9. to make a bargain; to come to terms; to compromise. 10. to settle a debt, claim, etc., by compromise.
2. _____	*verb (used with an object)* 1. to offer to view; to present for inspection: 2. to display. 3. to place on show. 4. to explain. 5. Law. to submit (a document, object, etc.) in evidence in a court of law. *verb (used without an object)* 6. to present something to public view. *noun* 7. an act or instance of showing for public view. 8. something that is shown for public view. 9. an object or a collection of objects shown in public. 10. Law. a document or object shown in court and referred to and identified in written evidence.
3. _____	*noun* 1. a choice limited to one of two or more possibilities. 2. one of the things or courses of action that can be chosen. 3. a possible or remaining course or choice. *adjective* 4. affording a choice of two or more things. 5. of two things so that if one is chosen the other must be rejected. 6. employing or following ideas, methods, etc. that are not traditional; existing outside what is considered proper or normal. 7. Logic. (of a proposition) asserting two or more choices, at least one of which is true.

Unit 8: Dancing Until You Drop **55**

Vocabulary Reinforcement

A. Complete the passage using the given words. Three words will NOT be used.

validity	abnormal	compounded
exhibit	participates	alternatives
civil	psychological	regions

A person who seeks 1. _____ help from professionals may, upon entering the system, be labeled "normal" or "2. _____." While in some cases there is 3. _____ in applying such labels, not all cases can be so easily diagnosed. The definition of what is normal or not normal is not the same across all 4. _____ of the world. People who travel between countries may appear strange in foreign lands if they 5. _____ normal behavior from their homelands. Perhaps it is time to consider 6. _____ in how we define and label what is normal.

B. Fill in the blanks with the correct phrases. Three phrases will NOT be used.

exhibit symptoms	environmental event	rational thinking
compounded by	psychological stress	doubt the validity
participate in	behaving abnormally	

1. I need to take my dog to the veterinarian because she is _____.

2. There is not a lot of _____ in cases of mass hysteria.

3. After a person has gone through a lot of _____, he or she may act differently than normal.

4. Doctors sometimes _____ of patients' responses to questions about how much they drink.

5. Even when people are sick, they don't always _____ or feel unwell.

56 Psychology

Unit 9 Literature: Creative Writing

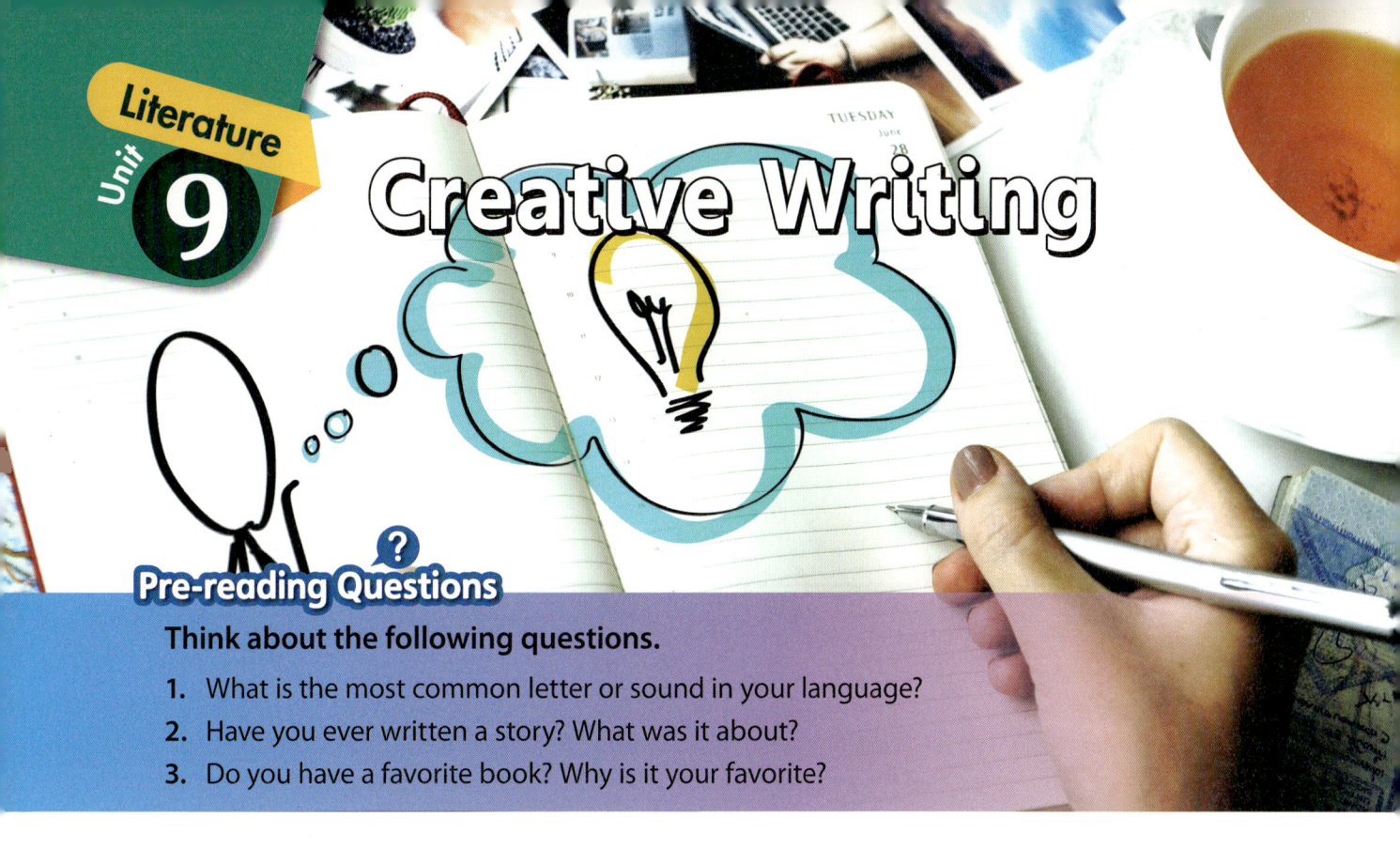

Pre-reading Questions

Think about the following questions.

1. What is the most common letter or sound in your language?
2. Have you ever written a story? What was it about?
3. Do you have a favorite book? Why is it your favorite?

Vocabulary Preview

Write the word that matches the definition.

structure	conceive	edition	classic
exclude	disposal	criteria	constrained
impose	initial	creative	document

1. one of a series of printings of the same book — n. _____
2. limited or restricted — adj. _____
3. the power or right to use or control — n. _____
4. to imagine; to think of — v. _____
5. to keep out; to remove from consideration — v. _____
6. able to make new things or think of new ideas — adj. _____
7. to frame or form something according to a plan — v. _____
8. a writing showing information; a paper with writing on it — n. _____
9. standards or rules for judging something — n. _____
10. to force someone to accept (something or yourself) — v. _____
11. first; primary — adj. _____
12. a novel, poem, song, etc., considered one of the best of its kind — n. _____

Literature

Constrained Writing

Topic at a Glance

Writers most often write a book or a story because they have a special idea or some message they want to share with others. But for some writers, writing is like a puzzle—they try and make the words and sentences into a game. That's the idea behind constrained writing. In constrained writing, the author sets a special kind of rule to follow throughout the entire story or book. For example, an author might set herself a rule that every word in her story will start with the letter *n*. Or another writer might set a rule that each sentence will have exactly ten words. Constrained writing pushes the actual art of writing and storytelling to its limits.

"If youth, throughout all history, had had a champion to stand up for it; to show a doubting world that a child can think; and, possibly, do it practically; you wouldn't constantly run across folks today who claim that 'a child don't know anything.'"

Look closely at the long sentence above. Do you notice anything strange? Maybe you
5   don't notice anything because the strange thing is very hard to see at first. But if you look closely, you will notice that the letter *e* is not used. The letter *e* does not appear anywhere in the entire sentence. This is unusual because the letter *e* is the most common letter in the English alphabet. In fact, the letter *e* is the most commonly used letter in Spanish, Italian, and French as well.

10   That sentence is the first line from a book published in 1939 called *Gadsby*. The book was **conceived** and written by Ernest Vincent Wright. What makes this book special is that the entire book is written without using the letter *e*. Not one single word in the 50,110 words that make up the book features an *e*.

E. V. Wright spent over ten years writing
15   *Gadsby* because it was so difficult for him to **structure** sentences and ideas without words that contain an *e* at his **disposal**. He constantly had to go back and rewrite pages and change ideas because of his self-**imposed** limitation[1].

20   *Gadsby*, as a novel, was only average. It was not a bad book. But its plot about a small, tired town that gets its teenagers to help revive[2] the area and improve living standards for the residents was not very exciting to many readers. People bought the book mostly because of its unusual writing style. However, *Gadsby* quickly became forgotten. Not long after the
25   first **edition** came out, a fire burned down the warehouse[3] containing most of the copies

---

[1] limitation (n.) — a condition set as a restriction or boundary
[2] revive (v.) — to bring back to life or health
[3] warehouse (n.) — a building where a business stores commodities

of the novel. This made the book hard to find and made the few remaining copies rare and worth a lot of money. But E. V. Wright did not end up making much money from the book that took him so long to write. He died in the same year the book was published. After *Gadsby*, a French author wrote a book in French which also **excluded** use of the letter *e*. Though it had a more exciting story, people were not interested, and it did not sell very well either.

This type of writing used by Wright and the French author is called **constrained** writing, and it often involves leaving out a particular letter (usually *e* or *o*). There are other types of constrained writing that use different **criteria** as well. One type of constrained writing is the Japanese haiku[4]. Haiku is limited to three lines and follows a pattern of 5-7-5 syllables[5]. Children's author Dr. Seuss wrote a **classic** book called *Green Eggs and Ham* that only uses 50 different words in the entire story. And in 2004, another French author, Michel Thaler, wrote a 233-page novel that does not contain a single verb! This level of achievement[6] was considered to be the most difficult because verbs are necessary to show action or movement.

Constrained writing may not be very exciting to read, but many students who study English writing use it to be more **creative**. It forces writers to think of other ways to express their ideas. And it makes them look for other words that they may not have used or thought of before, which helps build their vocabulary.

So if you can overcome the **initial** difficulty of writing a **document** with certain limits, you could find that practicing constrained writing might open up a whole new world of writing. With or without the letter *e*.

[4] haiku (n.) — a type of Japanese poetry
[5] syllable (n.) — a part of a word with a single vowel sound in it
[6] achievement (n.) — something that was completed through great effort or courage

Reading Comprehension

Choose the best answer.

1. Why was *Gadsby* a difficult book to write?
    a. Not one word in the book has an *e* in it.
    b. The author did not know English.
    c. The plot was very complex and difficult to describe.
    d. The book was written half in French and half in English.

2. According to paragraph 5, all of the following are true about *Gadsby* EXCEPT
    a. Many copies of the book were burned in a fire.
    b. Wright died soon after the book came out.
    c. *Gadsby* was a very bad book.
    d. It was published before a French novel that was written with a similar constraint.

3. Why does the writer mention *Green Eggs and Ham* in paragraph 6?
    a. Because constrained writing is most often used in children's books
    b. Because the author of *Gadsby* and this children's book are the same person
    c. Because the author of this children's book also wrote under a constraint
    d. Because none of the words contain the letter *o*

4. What is meant by "practicing constrained writing might open up a whole new world of writing"?
    a. A writer can make new worlds through their writing.
    b. Constrained writing is a new technique in the world of writing.
    c. Every writer in the world uses constrained writing.
    d. Constrained writing could help you become a better writer.

Paraphrasing Practice

Find the sentence(s) from the given paragraph that means the same as the given sentence. Copy the sentence(s) from the paragraph.

1. **Paragraph 4** Because of the way he chose to write the book, Wright was always having to make a lot of changes.

    _____
    _____

2. **Paragraph 7** Sometimes constrained writing is not very interesting, but it can make people better writers.

    _____
    _____

60 Literature

Language Focus

> Follow *because* with a subject and verb to form a dependent clause. Follow *because of* with a noun phrase.
>
> ➧ Maybe you don't notice anything <u>because</u> the strange thing is very hard to see at first.
> ➧ People bought the book mostly <u>because of</u> its unusual writing style.

Read each sentence and decide if *of* should be added to the sentence where indicated.

1. Because (   ) verbs are necessary to show action or movement, it's an amazing achievement to write a story without any verbs.

2. Writers write books because (   ) ideas or messages that they want to share.

3. Because (   ) Wright's self-imposed limitation, he constantly had to rewrite pages.

4. Wright spent years writing his novel because (   ) structuring the story and explaining ideas were difficult using words without an *e* in them.

5. Writing a book without any words with the letter *e* in them is unusual because (   ) the high frequency of this letter in English words.

Vocabulary Extension

Review the vocabulary word card exercise of practicing words in two languages. Study words going from English to your first language and then from your first language to English.

Work with a partner. Choose any five words from the reading passage. Write the English words here. Can your partner tell you the words in his or her first language?

_____ _____ _____ _____ _____

Work with a partner who knows your first language. Choose any five words from the reading passage that you can translate into your language. Write the words in your language here. Can your partner tell you the words in English?

_____ _____ _____ _____ _____

Study Tip
Knowing the spoken form of the word helps learning. *Say the words aloud to yourself as you learn them.*

Unit 9: Creative Writing **61**

Vocabulary Reinforcement

A. Complete the passage using the given words. Three words will NOT be used.

structured	conceives	edition
classic	excluded	disposal
criteria	creative	document

A Clockwork Orange by Anthony Burgess is considered a **1.** _____ of the science fiction genre. Burgess used a **2.** _____ mix of English and Russian words in the story to create a familiar yet new language for his characters. The writer also **3.** _____ the story to show how greatly the main character changed in the end. However, Burgess's American publisher **4.** _____ the final chapter when printing the book. Burgess did not agree with doing this, but in the end, the American **5.** _____ was used by Stanley Kubrick when he made the movie. Filmgoers in England and Europe who had Burgess's novel with all chapters included at their **6.** _____ were confused by the movie. It seemed to end before the story was finished.

B. Fill in the blanks with the correct phrases. Three phrases will NOT be used.

the classic edition	structure the document	at my disposal
exclude certain criteria	level of achievement	conceived the possibility
self-imposed limitation	constrain my creativity	

1. The same branch of the store held the highest _____ in sales for five years in a row.

2. Many people from civilized European cities _____ of living in the Wild West of America in the 1800s as exciting and filled with opportunity.

3. In order to _____ in your search results, use the word *not* in your search list.

4. This version of the game is fun, but I really prefer _____ of the game.

5. You can find examples online that will show you good ways to _____ that you were asked to write.

Unit 10 Literature: Personal Narratives

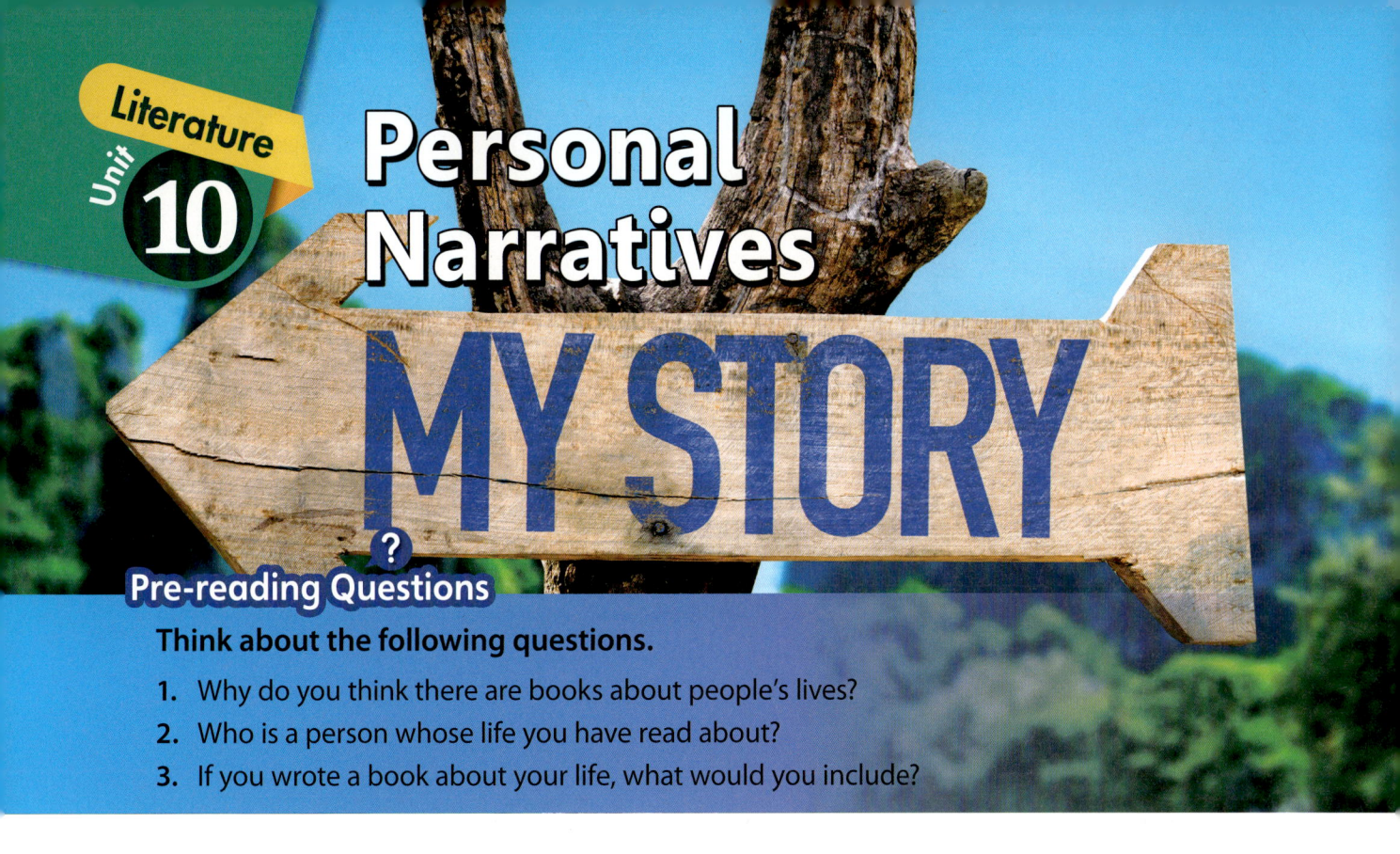

MY STORY

Pre-reading Questions

Think about the following questions.

1. Why do you think there are books about people's lives?
2. Who is a person whose life you have read about?
3. If you wrote a book about your life, what would you include?

Vocabulary Preview

Write the word that matches the definition.

incapable	category	chapter	circumstance
distinct	found	investigate	ongoing
perspective	publication	release	vehicle

1. a section of a book — n. _____
2. to carry out a formal study; to research — v. _____
3. a group of things that have shared characteristics — n. _____
4. continuing — adj. _____
5. a condition connected to an event or action — n. _____
6. the action of making a product available for viewing or purchase — n. _____
7. not having the ability — adj. _____
8. the process of putting out a book for sale — n. _____
9. clearly different from something else — adj. _____
10. a particular attitude toward something — n. _____
11. to establish or start — v. _____
12. a channel or means — n. _____

Biographies, Autobiographies, Memoirs Galore

Topic at a Glance

The stories of people's lives are interesting. These stories offer insight into different times of history as the stories bring history alive. These stories also provide windows into different areas of interest such as science, sports, medicine, politics, and art, to name a few. Additionally, these stories give a fresh perspective on a person's experiences or how a person views the world uniquely through his or her own eyes.

There are many **categories** of books that focus on the lives of real people, but the three that are typically associated with personal stories are biographies[1], autobiographies[2], and memoirs[3]. These three types of writing are very similar in two important ways. First, they are nonfiction. This means that they are based on real-life events and the stories
5 are true. Second, the stories are about people's lives. For these two reasons, some places that sell books put these types of books in the same category. However, there are key differences that make these written forms of personal narratives **distinct** from each other.

Biographies tell about the life of someone other than the author. The author spends a great deal of time and effort **investigating** the person's life. In a sense, it is similar
10 to reporting because the author may interview people who knew or encountered the subject of the book personally. One example of a famous biography is *Steve Jobs,* which was written by Walter Isaacson at Steve Jobs's request. To write the biography, Isaacson interviewed Jobs forty times over the course of two years and interviewed more than one hundred people who knew Jobs. The result was a 42-**chapter**, 656-page biography
15 that told the story of Steve Jobs's life from his childhood to his death at 55 years of age. When the book was **released** just nineteen days after his death, it was a top-seller in the US, with 379,000 copies sold in its first week. It has also been translated into quite a few languages and proven popular around the world. This may be because many
20 people were interested in the life and person of Steve Jobs, most famously known as one of the men who **founded** Apple Inc. and revolutionized the industry of modern technology. Jobs was adopted[4] at birth, half-Arab, a Buddhist, and a college dropout[5]—all intriguing

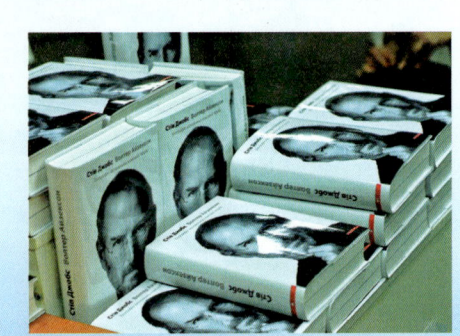

---

[1] biography (n.) — a book written about a person's life
[2] autobiography (n.) — a book written by one about one's own life
[3] memoir (n.) — a book written about a person using information from shared experiences
[4] adopt (v.) — to take as one's child a child who is not one's own by birth
[5] dropout (n.) — a person who quits school before graduating

64 Literature

aspects about Jobs that made him even more interesting to read about.

Autobiographies and biographies are similar in that they tell the story of a person's life; the key difference is that the author and the subject in an autobiography are the same. A famous autobiography is Mahatma Gandhi's *The Story of My Experiments with Truth*. Mahatma Gandhi is most well known for leading India's independence[6] movement through nonviolent civil disobedience[7]. Though he thought the writing of an autobiography was a Western practice, his co-workers encouraged him to write one. Gandhi began writing the story of his life in an effort to narrate the background of his spiritual and moral experiments to understand truth. He wrote about his life from childhood to 1921, and his words were published in weekly articles for an **ongoing** period from 1925 to 1929. With the translation and **publication** of his autobiography into English in 1940, Gandhi has continued to inspire many readers with his words of wisdom and truth, such as, "What barrier is there that love cannot break?" and "Men often become what they believe themselves to be. If I believe I cannot do something, it makes me **incapable** of doing it. But when I believe I can, then I acquire the ability to do it even If I didn't have it in the beginning."

The final type of personal narrative is the memoir. Memoirs and autobiographies are similar in that the author and subject are the same. Therefore, the memoir is written from the author's point of view. However, memoirs do not retell[8] all of the important events in the author's life. Instead, memoirs usually focus on a theme or single aspect of the author's life that are selected for the purpose of the book. Themes in memoirs are typically experiences that led to life lessons or a key experience that changed the way the author viewed the world. In writing a memoir, the author also hopes that the reader will gain a new **perspective** on the world as well. Another difference is that memoirs, though nonfiction, are usually written in a story form like fiction. One such famous memoir is Elie Wiesel's *Night*. In this book, published in 1958, Elie Wiesel narrates the stories of his experience as a young boy in Nazi concentration camps during World War II. He describes the struggle to survive in the extreme conditions as well as the struggle to understand his **circumstances**. This struggle included the boy's questioning of God and how and why God would allow such things to happen.

Biographies, autobiographies, and memoirs are all **vehicles** that give the reader an opportunity to walk in someone else's shoes—to take a journey through someone's life and gain a new perspective on people, events, and the world.

[6] independence (n.) — freedom
[7] disobedience (n.) — not following a known rule or law
[8] retell (v.) — to explain or say again

Reading Comprehension

Choose the best answer.

1. According to the passage, all of the following are true EXCEPT
   a. The author and subject are the same in an autobiography.
   b. Biographies, autobiographies, and memoirs are all considered to contain true events.
   c. Biographies are published after a person's death.
   d. The author and subject are the same in a memoir.

2. What does the term "adopted" in paragraph 2 refer to?
   a. Received special recognition
   b. Taken up to use
   c. Formally approve
   d. Taken as a part of a family legally

3. Why does the author provide quotes from Gandhi's autobiography in the passage?
   a. To give examples of his inspirational words
   b. To demonstrate that he was a nonviolent leader
   c. To imply that he loved everyone
   d. To suggest that he was a capable person

4. What can be inferred from paragraph 4?
   a. Wiesel's life after World War II was not interesting.
   b. Wiesel went through a difficult time as a child.
   c. Wiesel fought in World War II.
   d. Wiesel always wanted to write about his life.

Paraphrasing Practice

Find the sentence(s) from the given paragraph that means the same as the given sentence. Copy the sentence(s) from the paragraph.

1. **Paragraph 1** While all forms of personal narratives are fundamentally similar, they can be categorized into three distinct forms.

   _____
   _____

2. **Paragraph 2** Jobs's upbringing and life make him a fascinating person to read about.

   _____
   _____

Language Focus

The phrase be + "similar in that" should be followed by a clause containing a subject and verb.

➤ Autobiographies and biographies <u>are similar in that</u> they tell the story of a person's life.
➤ Memoirs and autobiographies <u>are similar in that</u> the author and subject are the same.

Match the parts to make correct sentences.

1. The three types are similar in that (   )
2. Researching a biography and (   ) reporting are similar in that
3. Thoreau and Gandhi were similar in that (   )
4. The books *Night* and *A Lucky Child* (   )

a. both rely on interviews.
b. each sought political change.
c. they are all nonfiction.
d. they tell the stories of children in concentration camps.

Vocabulary Extension

Hint: A common ending for verb word forms is *-ish*.

Complete the chart.

Noun	Verb	Adjective	Adverb
foundation	found	1.	—
publication	2.	published	—
capability	—	3.	capably
4.	—	circumstantial	circumstantially
punishment	5.	punishable	—
distinction	6.	distinct	distinctly

Unit 10: Personal Narratives **67**

Vocabulary Reinforcement

A. Complete the passage using the given words. Three words will NOT be used.

capable	category	chapters
circumstances	distinct	investigating
perspective	publication	released

Among the vast number of biographies, autobiographies, and memoirs published year after year, only a few have remained 1. _____ and can be called "the best of the best" in this 2. _____ of literature. What makes these books stand out? It is how the retelling of the 3. _____ of these people's lives in story form is 4. _____ of moving and inspiring readers around the world. For example, Benjamin Franklin's autobiography was 5. _____ hundreds of years ago, but people still enjoy the interesting 6. _____ of history written in Franklin's creative style.

B. Fill in the blanks with the correct phrases. Three phrases will NOT be used.

distinct perspective	ongoing investigation	released for publication
vehicle for sharing	categorized into sublists	circumstances of the encounter
another chapter	founded a journal	

1. The _____ between the author and the singer were concealed from the press.

2. In addition to language, art can serve as a(n) _____ thoughts and feelings.

3. Having lived in ten different countries, he has a _____ on life.

4. The author's latest horror novel was _____ the day before Halloween.

5. Due to the _____, a final decision in the case has not been reached.

Unit 11 Business: Office Hours

Pre-reading Questions

Think about the following questions.

1. Do you have a job? If so, how many hours do you work in a day?
2. What do you think is the best number of hours to work in a day? Why?
3. What do you think is the most important aspect about work?

Vocabulary Preview

Write the word that matches the definition.

emphasis	flexibility	implement	internal
margin	relevant	promote	shift
stress	suspend	trace	voluntarily

1. out of one's own free will — adv. _____
2. to describe the origin or development of — v. _____
3. the ability to be easily changed to fit different circumstances — n. _____
4. a state of mental or emotional strain — n. _____
5. on the inside — adj. _____
6. to support or actively encourage — v. _____
7. to prevent from continuing — v. _____
8. special importance or value given to something — n. _____
9. closely connected or appropriate to the matter at hand — adj. _____
10. to put into effect; to execute — v. _____
11. a period of work — n. _____
12. an amount by which a thing is won or falls short — n. _____

Origins of the 8-Hour Work Day

Topic at a Glance

Scientists often refer to the human body's internal clock as our circadian rhythm. It is the body's sleep-wake cycle that is roughly 24 hours. Based on circadian rhythm and other factors, experts have developed the ideal number of hours that people should sleep each day. On average, they recommend eight hours a day for adults. The circadian rhythm does not only regulate sleep, though. It also regulates how alert we are when awake. Knowing this can improve efficiency in how days are spent working and playing.

In most companies today, the eight-hour work day and 40-hour work week are typical. However, this was not always the case. Those working in agriculture[1] or in factories during the Industrial[2] Revolution of the 18th century operated on a "sun up, sun down" work day. This meant that not only were work days typically 10-16 hours or longer, but
5   work was also often 6 days a week. Even in the *Factories Act* of 1847 (an act that was **implemented** to standardize and improve working conditions), women and children still had 10-hour work days. The wages[3] in most factories were so low that workers had to work
10 long **shifts** in order to provide for their families. But it was all for nothing. The work day was both so long and difficult that workers could not work effectively or efficiently. Workers were also rarely happy under such conditions.

15 The idea of the eight-hour work day can be **traced** back to Britain's Robert Owen. He is known for making and **promoting** the phrase "Eight hours labor, eight hours recreation[4], eight hours rest" in 1817. Workers in the United States at the time were also holding strikes demanding eight-hour work days. Though this idea was supported by the working class, business owners were slow to change. Finally in 1914, Henry Ford **voluntarily suspended**
20 the ten-hour work day, implemented the eight-hour work day in his factories, and doubled the workers' pay. Ford's reason for the eight-hour work day or forty-hour work week wasn't so much out of kindness. In fact, he still expected the same amount of output from his workers even in a shorter day. Fair enough. Ford's goal was to increase efficiency and productivity into a shorter work day. The **emphasis** in Ford's factories was not on the
25 number of hours worked but on the amount of production achieved in a day. The results

---

[1] agriculture (n.) — farming; growing food to eat
[2] industrial (adj.) — related to the making of products for sale
[3] wage (n.) — the money a person earns for some amount of work
[4] recreation (n.) — play; any way that free time is enjoyed

were shocking. Not only did productivity increase, but so did Ford's profit **margins**. The Ford factory was so big and well-known at the time, the results of this change encouraged other factories and companies to implement the same concept of the eight-hour work day. Finally, in 1937, the United States standardized[5] the eight-hour work day in the Fair Labor Standards Act. The idea of the eight-hour work day has since spread to many countries, such as Iran, France, Russia, Germany, Mexico, and Spain, to name a few.

In the early twentieth century, the shorter work day had a huge impact on increasing worker productivity and on improving the quality of life of workers. Awesome[6]! However, today businesses are taking a second look at the eight-hour work day. Some say that, though it was an effective and humane[7] measure for workers back then, it is not **relevant** for today's workers. Some would argue that simply making the work day shorter is not enough to increase worker efficiency, productivity, and happiness. For example, everyone has a circadian rhythm, an **internal** clock; however, each person's circadian rhythm varies. There are those who work well early in the morning and those who work better starting later in the morning. More often than not, though, managers will tend to assume that those who start work late and end late are lazier, less productive, or less driven than their co-workers who start work early. Really? Interestingly, experts have found that **flexibility** in workers' schedules not only increases productivity, but also decreases worker **stress** and absence[8]. When employees are free to work when they are most alert, they work at their best. In addition, the brain cannot work continuously through an eight-hour work day. However, this is what seems to happen in most workplaces—workers will fight through times of low energy and continue to work. Scientists claim that the human mind can focus on a task for 90-120 minutes, after which the mind needs a 20-30 minute break. Only when the mind is able to function according to this cycle of work and rest is it able to maintain a high level of performance.

Some companies have shifted their thought to managing worker energy level rather than managing worker time. And why not? For example, Google has added special places in the office for taking naps at work. Other companies have exercise rooms, play rooms, and cafés where their workers can relax. Each has found that with these changes, worker productivity, creativity, and happiness have increased. The current trends of flexible schedules and managing workers' energy levels appear to be the next step in moving beyond the eight-hour work day toward new levels of worker productivity and satisfaction.

[5] standardize (v.) — to make the same for all people or all situations
[6] awesome (adj.) — great; terrific
[7] humane (adj.) — showing care for people or animals
[8] absence (n.) — not being where something or someone should be

Reading Comprehension

Choose the best answer.

1. According to the passage, all of the following are true EXCEPT
   a. Workers had very long hours in the 18th and 19th century.
   b. The mind needs a break from periods of concentration longer than 90-120 minutes.
   c. Circadian rhythm refers to a standardized world clock.
   d. Companies today promote measures to increase workplace satisfaction and production.

2. Why does the author mention Robert Owen?
   a. He changed the work laws in Britain.
   b. He was famous for suggesting a balanced day of work, play, and rest.
   c. He ran a big factory that reduced the working hours for its workers.
   d. He opposed changing the working conditions in Britain.

3. What can be inferred from paragraph 2?
   a. Henry Ford was a man who cared more about his workers than his company.
   b. Henry Ford was a forward-thinking man who changed the way people think about work.
   c. People became lazier with the shorter work day.
   d. A few countries have eight-hour work days currently; most still have 10-16 hour work days.

4. What does the term "fight" in paragraph 3 refer to?
   a. To take part in a violent struggle
   b. To attempt to put out a fire
   c. To move forward with difficulty
   d. To campaign against something

Paraphrasing Practice

Find the sentence(s) from the given paragraph that means the same as the given sentence. Copy the sentence(s) from the paragraph.

1. **Paragraph 2** People in the US agreed with the idea of shorter work shifts and wanted eight-hour working days to be the norm.

   _____

   _____

2. **Paragraph 3** Work flexibility and breaks allow for increased productivity and decreased stress in the workplace.

   _____

   _____

72 Business

Unit 11 Business

Language Focus

Sentence fragments can be used for several reasons: (1) in a description, (2) for transition, (3) for indicating conclusions, (4) in leading to an example or an answer, (5) for making exclamations, and (6) for making explanations.

➡ Some companies have shifted their thought to managing worker energy level rather than managing worker time. <u>And why not?</u> For example, Google has added special places in the office for taking naps at work. (Use of fragment: in leading to an example)

Underline the sentence fragment in the given sentences. Then write the function of the fragment choosing from the six options above.

1. In the early twentieth century, the shorter work day had a huge impact on increasing worker productivity and on improving the quality of life of workers. Awesome! However, today businesses are taking a second look at the eight-hour work day.

   Use of fragment _____

2. In fact, he still expected the same amount of output from his workers even in a shorter day. Fair enough. Ford's goal was to increase efficiency and productivity into a shorter work day.

   Use of fragment _____

3. More often than not, though, managers will tend to assume that those who start work late and end late are lazier, less productive, or less driven than their coworkers who start work early. Really? Interestingly, experts have found that flexibility in workers' schedules not only increases productivity, but also decreases worker stress and absence.

   Use of fragment _____

Vocabulary Extension

Write the words below with the same suffixes together as a group. What do you think is the function of each suffix? Check the function in the appendix.

| acceptance | awesome | business | creativity | emptiness | endurance |
| forgiveness | inability | lonesome | performance | productivity | troublesome |

Group 1	Group 2	Group 3	Group 4

suffix 1: _____   suffix 2: _____   suffix 3: _____   suffix 4: _____

function: _____   function: _____   function: _____   function: _____

Unit 11: Office Hours 73

Vocabulary Reinforcement

A. Complete the passage using the given words. Three words will NOT be used.

stress	suspended	wages
emphasis	flexibility	implement
margins	promote	shifts

Many businesses schedule 1. _____ that change every day or every week. This may lead to extra 2. _____ in a person's life because he or she can't predict which hours will be taken up by work on a given day. It has been suggested that companies should 3. _____ a policy of two-week advance notice for all workers' schedules. On top of that, if set schedules change, the 4. _____ that workers normally receive should reflect some small compensation for their 5. _____ in changing their off-work schedules to meet work demands. Both suggestions here 6. _____ workplace practices that, in the end, benefit employees as well as employers.

B. Fill in the blanks with the correct phrases. Three phrases will NOT be used.

the night shift	higher wages	emphasis on recreation
flexible class schedules	trace the path	relevant symptom
internal stress	a margin for error	

1. He decided to work _____ during the holidays.

2. Janice was dealing with a lot of _____ due to pressures at work, home, and school.

3. The school implemented _____ to accommodate working students.

4. I learned some new skills at summer camp, but really the camp had a(n) _____ over study.

5. A promotion at work usually comes with _____ as well.

Unit 12 Business: Management Styles

Pre-reading Questions

Think about the following questions.

1. Have you ever been the leader of a group of people?
2. What happens when a group has a bad leader?
3. What qualities do you think make a good leader?

Vocabulary Preview

Write the word or phrase that matches the definition.

consultant	welfare	grant	incorporated
institute	parameter	odd	stability
on one's behalf	instruction	insight	accommodation

1. a limit or boundary; a guideline — n. _____
2. strange; not expected — adj. _____
3. to begin a rule or process that others must follow — v. _____
4. a person who gives professional advice to companies for a fee — n. _____
5. made part of; combined with others into one body — adj. _____
6. to give control; to allow — v. _____
7. adjustments or allowances to meet everyone's wants or needs — n. _____
8. deep or clear understanding of something — n. _____
9. in the interest of; for the benefit of — idiom _____
10. information about how to do something — n. _____
11. the state of being firm or not likely to fall — n. _____
12. well-being; the happiness and health of a person or group — n. _____

The Art of Management

Topic at a Glance

Working for a large company is the goal of many students when they graduate from college. They hope that after a few years they can rise up through the ranks and become managers someday. However, many people don't think about the different styles of managing people. Why is it that some bosses are respected by their workers while others are not? Why are some companies better at keeping good employees while others can't seem to keep people around for very long? Whether the company is famous around the world or just a small business of a few people, the management style can go a long way in determining whether the business will be successful or not.

Any business or company that has workers probably has at least one manager to oversee[1] both employees and productivity. Some people think that being a manager, or a boss, is just about telling people what to do—and getting angry when they don't do it. But being a good manager is a lot more than that. Good bosses bring out the best in their employees. They make their employees work, but more importantly they get their employees to want to work because they feel valued and important to the company.

So how does a person learn to manage others? John Slestack, a business **consultant** for many world-famous companies, says that there are three different types of management styles: autocratic[2], democratic[3], and free-reign[4].

Autocratic managers make decisions by themselves. They don't ask for ideas or suggestions from their workers. These types of bosses think that they know what is best for the company and expect their workers to follow the rules and decisions that they **institute**. This type of management style is sometimes good and sometimes bad. It is good when there are a lot of new employees who don't know all of the **parameters** of their job well, or when decisions need to be made quickly because of a deadline[5]. However, most of the time autocratic managers are not liked by their employees. In most cases, when bosses make decisions by themselves, it makes the workers feel that their ideas don't have any value. They feel like robots that can easily be replaced, and they don't try to work hard at their jobs.

---

[1] oversee (v.) — to watch and control as a boss or manager
[2] autocratic (adj.) — having complete power
[3] democratic (adj.) — ensuring that all people have equal power
[4] free-reign (adj.) — giving freedom to do as one wishes
[5] deadline (n.) — the time or date by which something must be finished

Democratic managers make decisions with input from other people. They seek out the **insight** of others and ask for suggestions on how to do things. They listen to the thoughts and words of their workers. This type of management style also has both good and bad points. It is the most liked style of management reported by workers; they feel that democratic managers listen to what they have to say and care about their **welfare** in the workplace. As a result, they try to do the best job that they can on the company's **behalf**. There can be downsides[6] as well. Sometimes it is not possible to ask around to collect every employee's suggestion or make **accommodations** for each person's ideas. And there are times when a deadline has to be met and there is not time to meet with everyone and get their input.

The third type of management style is called free-reign. Free-reign managers take a back seat role in the daily operations[7] of the office, giving guidance[8] only when needed or asked for. Employees are **granted** the freedom to come up with their own ideas and express creativity in their jobs. Most people might think that this type of management style is the one most appreciated by employees…but that's not true. **Odd** as it may seem, most workers do not like this style of management at all! Why? Because most workers feel that to do their job the best, they need a good leader to provide guidance and **stability** to the team. It may be fun for a little while, but if no one is in charge, workers feel like people will just do whatever they want to do. Furthermore, free-reign management is cited as one reason that employee production goes down.

So even though each style has its good and bad points, the management style that is usually most effective is the democratic style. Workers want to have a manager who provides some **instruction** for them, but they want a manager who also values their opinion and ideas. They want to feel like they are **incorporated** into a team with their colleagues and manager, and not like they are just machines doing what others program them to do.

Remember this if you rise through the ranks and become a manager someday. There are times to be strong and make decisions for those you are managing. And there are times to stand back and let employees manage themselves. But certainly all of the time, it is best to treat people with respect. Be flexible and lead while listening to others.

---

[6] downside (n.) — a negative result or aspect

[7] operations (n.) — all of the things that must normally be done to keep a company running

[8] guidance (n.) — instruction; information to lead others in the correct way

Unit 12: Management Styles

Reading Comprehension

Choose the best answer.

1. What is the meaning of "Good bosses bring out the best in their employees" in paragraph 1?
   a. Good bosses only hire the best workers.
   b. Good bosses make their workers want to do their best.
   c. Good bosses bring their best employees out to lunch.
   d. Good bosses make their best employees work harder than other workers.

2. Why does the author mention new employees in paragraph 3?
   a. To show which workers will make bad managers
   b. Because new employees are most likely to make managers angry
   c. To explain who might work best under democratic management
   d. As an example of a group that might need autocratic management

3. According to the last paragraph, all are true about managing people EXCEPT
   a. It is good to treat people with respect.
   b. Good managers sometimes listen to their employees.
   c. You should never let workers manage themselves.
   d. Sometimes bosses have to make decisions without asking other people.

4. What is meant by the phrase "rise through the ranks" in the last paragraph?
   a. To become more autocratic as in a military style
   b. To quit your job and work for a different company
   c. To make a request for change to an authority higher than your boss
   d. To keep getting promotions until someday you are a manager

Paraphrasing Practice

Find the sentence(s) from the given paragraph that means the same as the given sentence. Copy the sentence(s) from the paragraph.

1. **Paragraph 4** Democratic managers ask other people for their opinions and ideas before making a decision.

   _____

   _____

2. **Paragraph 5** Free-reign managers don't tell people what to do unless that person comes to them with a problem.

   _____

   _____

78 Business

Language Focus

A phrasal verb is a combination of a verb and particle (preposition, adverb, or adverb plus preposition). The particle changes the meaning of the phrasal verb in idiomatic ways.

➡ Good bosses bring out the best in their employees.
➡ Employees are granted the freedom to come up with their own ideas.

Fill in the blanks with the correct phrasal verb from the box.

| ask around | care about | feel like | seek out | stand back |

1. Some managers _____ the insight of others and ask for suggestions on how to do things.

2. There are times when managers need to _____ and let employees manage themselves.

3. Sometimes it is not possible to _____ to collect every employee's suggestion.

4. Employees want to _____ they are incorporated into a team with their colleagues and manager.

5. Democratic managers listen to what employees have to say and _____ their welfare in the workplace.

Vocabulary Extension

Read the example sentences and the definitions for the underlined words. Then choose the best core meaning to match the underlined words.

1. a. He had a role as a detective in the movie.   (an actor's character)
   b. Her role in the company is CEO.   (a job in a group or company)
   c. The roles of parents have changed over the years. (a duty in society)

   role   looks / part / side

2. a. Our guide led us through the jungle.   (one who shows the way)
   b. The pilot will guide the airplane landing.   (to direct or control)
   c. I didn't read my new phone's user's guide.   (instruction book)

   guide   lead / manage / rule

Unit 12: Management Styles **79**

Vocabulary Reinforcement

A. Complete the passage using the given words. Three words will NOT be used.

parameters	odd	incorporated
insight	accommodations	consultant
welfare	grant	institute

A person who enjoys solving problems and working with others might want to work as a management **1.** _____. Both big and small companies turn to such consultants for **2.** _____ into solving their biggest problems. Maybe they are asked to help set **3.** _____ for new technology systems or to provide detailed instruction when building a new company website. The challenge for management consultants is finding **4.** _____ for a company's needs, budget, and deadlines in the solutions they hope to **5.** _____. Of course, a critical skill that must be **6.** _____ with a consultant's skill for problem solving is his or her skill in communication.

B. Fill in the blanks with the correct phrases. Three phrases will NOT be used.

grant accommodation	lacked stability	incorporated the parameters
institute new rules	a welfare program	odd instructions
on behalf of	the consultant's insight	

1. Andrew will attend the meeting _____ his manager because she is sick.

2. Due to complaints from last year's competition, we will _____ in the company soccer tournament this year.

3. I was suspicious of the email because I didn't recognize the sender and it had some _____ in it.

4. The children grew up without much guidance from their parents and _____ in their lives.

5. Using the results from their study, the company _____ into their plan for marketing products in Africa.

Unit 13 Music: The Root of Modern Opera

Pre-reading Questions

Think about the following questions.

1. What is a show, play, or opera you have seen on the stage?
2. What are some famous operas you have heard of?
3. Who are some famous opera composers?

Vocabulary Preview

Write the word that matches the definition.

confine	maintain	summarize	radical
consistent	interpret	logical	attain
notion	cease	restraint	subordinate

1. to keep at a given level; to continue as something is — v. _____
2. according to reason; as expected by reliable thinking — adj. _____
3. to make less than or secondary; to place under — v. _____
4. agreeing with other parts; holding together in a logical way — adj. _____
5. to reach a goal; to accomplish a desired result — v. _____
6. an idea; a way of thinking — n. _____
7. to explain or tell the meaning of — v. _____
8. extremely different — adj. _____
9. to stop — v. _____
10. the act of showing control or holding back — n. _____
11. to keep in a limited area; to hold within certain parameters — v. _____
12. to express concisely — v. _____

Unit 13: The Root of Modern Opera 81

Music

The Composer You May Not Have Heard Of 🎵 14

Topic at a Glance

When you go to see a show on stage that is a story with singing in it, are you watching an opera or a musical? Musicals are usually defined as a stage story told through speech, song, and dance. Operas, on the other hand, are considered an art form in which musicians and singers use songs and music in telling a story. However, many modern stage shows blur the lines between musicals and operas. Perhaps a more useful way to understand the difference between musicals and operas is to consider who writes these shows. The writer of a musical is considered just that, a writer. An opera, though, is always written by a composer.

The composer Christoph Gluck achieved wide fame[1] in his own time. However, his works are rarely seen or heard in opera houses today. He is known today as a revolutionary composer who changed the approach of many who followed him. About his own work *Alceste*, Gluck wrote
5 that he "sought to **confine** music to its true function of serving poetry by expressing feelings and the situations of the story without interrupting and cooling off the action through useless and superfluous[2] ornaments." This statement has been **interpreted** by some as indicating
10 Gluck's desire to **subordinate** music to poetry. This actually seems far from the case. Gluck believed that music becomes more powerful and expressive[3] when it is balanced with the poetry of the words sung to it. In Gluck's works, one finds that music is used as a means of
15 **maintaining** the flow of the dramatic action of an opera rather than bringing the action to a stop while a singer performs an aria[4].

Audiences of his time recognized the power and beauty of Gluck's new approach to opera. In fact, in 1779, with the production of *Iphigenia in Tauris*, all of Paris immediately fell in love with this great work. Gluck's critics of that time were silenced in the wave of
20 enthusiasm[5] which swept the public. *Iphigenia in Tauris* may be the best example of Gluck's ability to use music to reflect the dramatic action within the story. While Orestes sings in the opera "My heart is calm," the orchestra paints a rather different understanding of his thoughts. Interestingly, during one rehearsal[6] the musicians failed to understand the

---

[1] fame (n.) — being well-known and well thought of by many people
[2] superfluous (adj.) — extra; not necessary
[3] expressive (adj.) — able to show thought or emotion
[4] aria (n.) — a solo song in an opera performed to music played by an orchestra
[5] enthusiasm (n.) — strong emotion that shows interest, usually in something new or different
[6] rehearsal (n.) — a time of practice before a public performance

connection of their playing to the singer's words and **ceased** playing. The composer yelled in anger at the orchestra, "Don't you see he is lying? Go on, go on!"

Gluck often said that while composing, he always tried to forget he was a musician. He entered the field of operatic composition when others of his time simply followed traditional dry forms, utterly[7] without soul and poetic spirit. Their objective seemed either to be to show audiences their understanding of musical forms or to give performers the opportunity to display their singing abilities. Opera as an art form for expressing human emotions, performed through a well-structured dramatic story, was completely beyond any composers' **notion** of the time. Early in his career, Gluck hit upon the **radical** idea that opera could be used to show art rather than just be used to show off. However, it took him many years to develop his musical ideas according to a theory, and he never carried that theory to the **logical** conclusion. That job would fall to Wagner, who composed his great operas in the 1800s. Still, Gluck accomplished much in the way of changing the way composers understood operatic composition. He carefully fashioned the singing to serve as explanatory[8] elements in opera, and he insisted that his singers should make these elements the object of their most careful musical efforts. Additionally, other parts of the opera—the arias, duos, quartets, etc., as well as the choruses and orchestral parts—were made **consistent** with the dramatic situations and motivations of the performers.

The principles of Gluck's school of operatic writing may be briefly **summarized** according to the following points. First, that dramatic music can only reach its highest power and beauty when it is joined to a simple and poetic text that expresses emotions true to Nature. Another key principle is that the music of an opera must exactly follow the rhythm and melody of the words. In addition, the orchestra must be used to build the power of the emotions expressed in the singing of the performers, as demanded by the text or dramatic situation.

Although few might hear them today, in Gluck's compositions for opera one finds a fine balance of music and poetry. It should also be noted how he composed with careful artistic **restraint**. His work consistently exhibits a simple and clear, yet also deep and rich style of composition. In fact, Gluck sought and **attained** the symmetrical[9] balance of an old Greek play.

[7] utterly (adv.) — completely
[8] explanatory (adj.) — relating to explaining or giving information
[9] symmetrical (adj.) — being the same on both sides

Unit 13: The Root of Modern Opera

Reading Comprehension

Choose the best answer.

1. How did audiences in the 1700s react to Gluck's *Iphigenia in Tauris*?
   a. They greeted it with enthusiasm.
   b. They ignored it because it was hard to understand.
   c. They showed dislike for it through silence.
   d. They thought it was superfluous.

2. Why did the orchestra stop playing during a rehearsal of *Iphigenia in Tauris*?
   a. The composer ordered them to stop.
   b. The musicians were confused.
   c. The orchestra was afraid of Gluck.
   d. The singer forgot the words to sing.

3. Which of the following is true according to the reading?
   a. Gluck and Wagner were not friendly due to their radical disagreement.
   b. Gluck refused to use songs in his operas to help explain the story.
   c. Gluck's work seems to lack soul and poetic spirit.
   d. Wagner improved on Gluck's ideas of operatic composition.

4. Which statement would Gluck probably have agreed with?
   a. Music is a powerful tool for expressing emotion.
   b. The orchestra is subordinate to the singer on the stage.
   c. The text of an opera loses poetic impact when it is sung.
   d. The true function of poetry is to confine emotions using words.

Paraphrasing Practice

Find the sentence(s) from the given paragraph that means the same as the given sentence. Copy the sentence(s) from the paragraph.

1. **Paragraph 1** When poetry is put to music, the power and expressive potential of music is enhanced.

   _____
   _____

2. **Paragraph 3** Although Gluck worked for years to create his theory of operatic composition, it was Wagner who showed the final logical application of these ideas.

   _____
   _____

Language Focus

> The word *rather* is an adverb meaning *quite* or *fairly*. The phrase *rather than* is used to talk about a preference of two things.
>
> ➭ The orchestra paints a <u>rather</u> different understanding of his thoughts.
> ➭ Gluck used music as a means of maintaining the flow of the dramatic action <u>rather than</u> bringing the action to a stop while a singer performs an aria.

Read each sentence and decide if *than* should be added to the sentence where indicated.

1. A shift in opera came when composers looked to Shakespeare or Goethe rather (   ) stories from Greek mythology for inspiration.

2. I had my doubts about the soprano chosen to play Carmen in the opera, but in the end she was rather (   ) good considering her age and lack of experience.

3. In opera, even simple instructions like "Open the door!" are sung rather (   ) spoken.

4. Rather (   ) trying to be realistic, the movements of performers in Chinese opera are meant to be symbolic.

5. The new production of *Tosca* is rather (   ) entertaining, even if it looks more like a musical than the traditional opera.

Vocabulary Extension

Review the vocabulary word card exercise of practicing words in two languages. Study words going from English to your first language and then from your first language to English.

Work with a partner. Choose any eight words from the reading passage. Write the English words here. Can your partner tell you the words in his or her first language?

_____   _____   _____   _____

_____   _____   _____   _____

Work with a partner who knows your first language. Choose any eight words from the reading passage that you can translate into your language. Write the words in your language here. Can your partner tell you the words in English?

_____   _____   _____   _____

_____   _____   _____   _____

Vocabulary Reinforcement

A. Complete the passage using the given words. Three words will NOT be used.

consistent	interpret	attained
cease	maintain	notion
confines	logical	radical

David Cope was a composer of operas before he turned to computer programming. By the age of 40, Cope had not 1. _____ great fame for his work composing, but he was successful enough to make a living from it. The problem was that he could not 2. _____ his musical creativity. In fact, he hit a creative brick wall at age 40. That was when Cope had the 3. _____ to write a computer program to help him come up with musical ideas. His first computer-generated musical pieces were not great, but he refused to 4. _____ in his efforts. Not long after that, Cope realized that his programming was not 5. _____ with the way composers actually work. Composers work from all that they know and hear and then 6. _____ this musical data in new ways. Using this idea, Cope has now created software that actually writes good music!

B. Fill in the blanks with the correct phrases. Three phrases will NOT be used.

a radical notion	a consistent performance	logical interpretation
maintain a balance	shows little restraint	attain proficiency
cease fire	summarize the points	

1. It takes years of practice to _____ in a second language.

2. One purpose of rehearsal is to achieve _____ for a production.

3. The media _____ in criticizing those holding political office.

4. Be sure to _____ that you want your reader to remember in the conclusion of your essay.

5. The idea that physical exercise was good for women was _____ in the 1800s.

86 Music

Unit 14 Music: The Connection Between Music and Language

Pre-reading Questions

Think about the following questions.

1. What is your favorite type of music?
2. How often do you listen to music?
3. What type of music do you listen to when you are happy? Sad? Angry?

Vocabulary Preview

Write the word that matches the definition.

complement	fundamental	bond	capacity
overlap	explicit	ongoing	apparent
enhance	data	sequence	component

1. the order in which things happen — (n.) _____
2. to have parts that are the same parts as something else — (v.) _____
3. the ability to do something — (n.) _____
4. seeming; noticeable — (adj.) _____
5. to improve something — (v.) _____
6. one of the parts of something — (n.) _____
7. continuing to happen — (adj.) _____
8. to join with something else and make it better — (v.) _____
9. very clear and complete, leaving no doubt of meaning — (adj.) _____
10. facts or information used to analyze something — (n.) _____
11. related to the basic structure of something — (adj.) _____
12. something that is shared between people and forms a connection between them — (n.) _____

Music, Language, and the Brain

Topic at a Glance

Music and language are two things that all cultures and people have in common. While each of them certainly differs, there are many more similarities between the two than there are differences. People use music and language to communicate with one another. The interesting thing is that researchers have discovered that language and music occur in the same parts of the brain. This has led many to believe that there is a good possibility that they are much more connected than anyone has realized.

Music can be found in all cultures in the world. It plays an important role in many societies. Because of this, it has long been called "the universal language of all mankind[1]." Recent research suggests that language and music not only **complement** each
5　other, but may actually be more connected than anyone has ever realized. They share the same **fundamental** building blocks. Both can be used as a way to communicate with others. There may also be a link between the two that suggests that music actually improves intellectual[2] and emotional **capacity** in children.

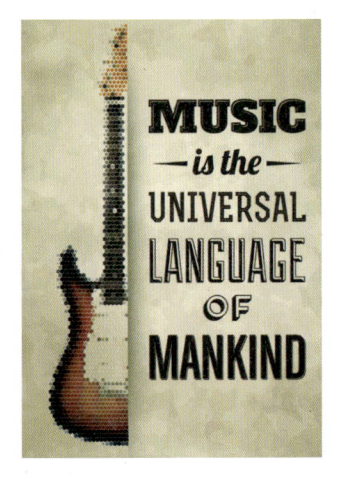

10　Music and language can be broken down into basic **components** and compared. They are compositional, meaning that they are made of small parts that can be used to create the meaning of something bigger. Language can be broken down into basic sounds, or phonemes, while music is made up of individual notes. Both music and language are symbolic and can be used to
15　communicate. They can also be read and written. The vocabulary of language is made up of different letters while music is made up of notes. Eight notes make up an octave[3], which can then be repeated at a lower or higher pitch. These notes can be arranged into measures in music, and many measures can create a piece. Similarly, words make up sentences, and sentences are used to create paragraphs.

20　Music and language also both have a certain logic and consistent[4] rules to them. Language has an order in which words can be arranged to make sense. By following these rules, words can be put together in an endless variety of ways. Understanding basic grammatical rules allows others to understand sentences they may have never heard before. This is important in communicating with others. Music also has rules for putting

---

[1] mankind (n.) — humans
[2] intellectual (adj.) — related to knowledge or learned facts
[3] octave (n.) — a series of eight tones or notes in a scale
[4] consistent (adj.) — agreeing; always following the same rule

notes in **sequences** that sound good together. There are also rules for stringing together sequences to create a melody[5]. However, this can vary, depending on the culture. Generally speaking, what is or is not acceptable in certain types of music appears to be more culturally based.

Both music and language have the ability to function in bringing people together. Language is used to communicate and to form social **bonds**. Music, likewise, can form bonds between people. Singing, such as a national anthem or hymns in church, can evoke[6] a strong sense of emotion and togetherness. This is especially true of group singing. The interesting thing about music is that it does not need to be **explicit** in order to be understood or send a message.

Scientists determined years ago that certain areas of the brain are responsible for language production and comprehension. **Ongoing** research suggests that music and language involve the same areas of the brain. The ability to comprehend and produce language is located in the Broca's area in the left hemisphere at the front of the brain. This area is also where knowledge of grammar is stored, which allows people to create sentences that makes sense to others. During brain scans, the Broca's area shows activity while listening to and interpreting speech and music.

While certain research has shown that music and language are processed using complex areas of the brain which **overlap**, other studies have shown an **apparent** link between music and higher IQ. Studies show the importance of using music to **enhance** learning. Children who study music before the age of seven have a better vocabulary and grammatical skills. Researchers believe that music helps students learn to recognize the differences between sounds and increases the ability to understand patterns within a language. **Data** shows that being able to understand sound patterns is helpful in learning how to read because it helps students connect sounds to the letters, characters, or symbols of their languages.

Connections made in the brain by allowing children to experience music early in life can help them solve problems unrelated to music. **Exposure** to music helps them grow and improve in reading, communicating, and interacting with others.

[5] melody (n.) — musical sounds that form part of a song
[6] evoke (v.) — to bring up; to make one feel, think of, or imagine

Reading Comprehension

Choose the best answer.

1. According to the passage, which of the following is true?
   a. Language is the best way to communicate emotions.
   b. Music has many more rules than language.
   c. Music and language activate the same area in the brain.
   d. It is best not to expose children to music.

2. Why does the author mention logic?
   a. Music is culturally biased.
   b. Music always creates social bonds.
   c. Music can only be understood when people interpret it in the same way.
   d. Music and language have consistent rules they follow.

3. According to the paragraph 6, which of the following is NOT true?
   a. There is a link between music and a higher IQ.
   b. Students who study music process grammar in both sides of their brains.
   c. Children who study music have better vocabulary skills.
   d. Understanding sound patterns helps children read.

4. According to the passage, is music important for children to learn? Why or why not?
   a. Yes, music helps kids improve in other areas of life.
   b. No, music makes children confuse rules of grammar.
   c. Yes, social bonds are even more important than language.
   d. No, music is only based on culture.

Paraphrasing Practice

Find the sentence(s) from the given paragraph that means the same as the given sentence. Copy the sentence(s) from the paragraph.

1. **Paragraph 3** Grammatical rules allow people to understand sentences they have never heard before and to communicate with others.

   _____

   _____

2. **Paragraph 6** Teaching music to children before they turn seven years old helps enhance vocabulary and grammatical skills.

   _____

   _____

Language Focus

> Non-action verbs are verbs that are typically not used in a progressive tense. Such verbs include the following: *appear, doubt, know, dislike, understand, suppose, agree, promise, involve, possess*, etc.
> - Certain types of music <u>appear</u> to be culturally based.
> - Ongoing research suggests that music and language <u>involve</u> the same areas of the brain.

Choose the correct form of the verb to complete each sentence.

1. I never (realized / was realizing) how closely connected language and music are.

2. Some sequences of notes naturally (sound / are sounding) good together.

3. We could see that the group (sing / was singing) with a strong sense of emotion.

4. While the brain (interpret / is interpreting) speech and music, the Broca's area will show activity.

5. Researchers (believe / are believing) that music helps students distinguish sounds and understand patterns within a language.

Vocabulary Extension

Write the words below with the same prefixes together as a group. What do you think each prefix means? Check the meaning in the appendix.

| concert | unfriendly | conspire | unicorn | convey | universal |
| disagree | unsafe | disappear | unrelated | dislike | unicellular |

Group 1	Group 2	Group 3	Group 4

prefix 1: _____   prefix 2: _____   prefix 3: _____   prefix 4: _____

meaning: _____   meaning: _____   meaning: _____   meaning: _____

Vocabulary Reinforcement

A. Complete the passage using the given words. Three words will NOT be used.

overlaps	sequence	apparent
bond	fundamental	capacity
enhance	data	component

There seems to exist strong evidence to support the claim that music has the 1. _____ to improve our minds. Musical training's ability to 2. _____ the development of math skills is 3. _____ when comparing test scores of music students to the scores of other students. But there also seems a(n) 4. _____ link between language and music. Research in verbal memory, second language learning, and reading all provide 5. _____ to support the notion that the way the brain processes music and language 6. _____.

B. Fill in the blanks with the correct phrases. Three phrases will NOT be used.

ongoing research	complement each other	social bonds
overlaps in areas	apparent link	fundamental building blocks
data shows	emotional capacity	

1. Phonemes are the _____ of language.

2. The function of processing music and language _____ of the brain.

3. Music is able to create _____ between people without using words.

4. Teaching music to children has been shown to increase their _____.

5. Research has found a(n) _____ between music and language.

Unit 15 Health: An Important Woman in Medicine

Pre-reading Questions

Think about the following questions.

1. What can doctors study to learn about health problems?
2. What do you know about cancer?
3. When do you think the first big breakthrough in cancer research was made?

Vocabulary Preview

Write the word that matches the definition.

assurance	undergo	consent	debate
distribution	ethical	extraction	medical
nonetheless	generate	enormous	minority

1. very great in size or amount — adj. _____
2. relating to treatment of disease or injuries — adj. _____
3. to experience or endure something — v. _____
4. to produce something — v. _____
5. the state of being sure or certain about something — n. _____
6. a small group of people who are different from others — n. _____
7. permission for something to be done — n. _____
8. the act of getting something by pulling it out — n. _____
9. involving questions of right and wrong — adj. _____
10. however; in spite of that — adv. _____
11. the act of delivering something to people — n. _____
12. to discuss something with people whose opinions are different from your own — v. _____

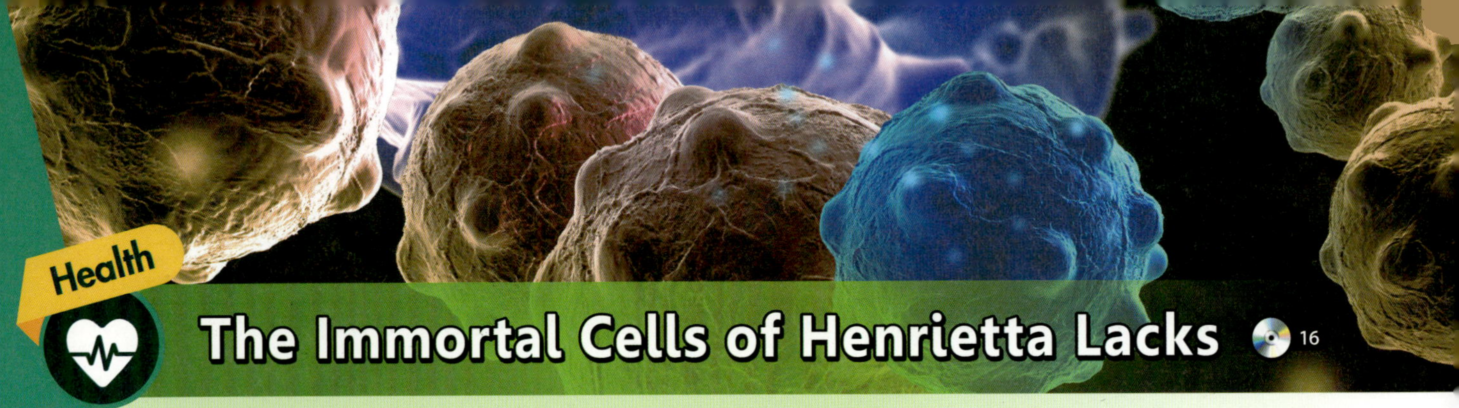

Health

The Immortal Cells of Henrietta Lacks

Topic at a Glance

In the 1950s, it was common for doctors and researchers to take samples of patients without their knowledge. Researchers were looking for human cells that could divide on their own endlessly outside the body. They finally found what they were looking for in the cancer cells of a woman named Henrietta Lacks. Her cells were taken without her knowledge and have since been used by thousands of researchers. Her family never received any compensation, though many large companies have made money off of her cells.

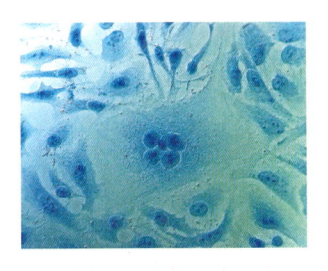

Medical researchers and doctors use cells in their work in order to test and treat various diseases. Cells are important because they are the basic building blocks for all living things. The human body is composed of trillions[1] of cells. But not all
5   cells need to be part of the body. Doctors have been able to grow cells outside the body since 1907. With normal cells growing outside the body, most can divide about 50 times before they die. Scientists were looking for a line of human cells that would live indefinitely[2] outside the body; however, they just couldn't keep cells alive beyond a certain point. That changed in the 1950s. There
10   is one woman to thank for a number of scientific breakthroughs[3] and practices over the last half century. Her "immortal[4]" cells were cultured upon initial **extraction** and have been dividing and growing in labs worldwide since then.

    Henrietta Lacks was a black woman from Virginia who felt a hard place in her lower stomach for a very long time before deciding to go to
15   Johns Hopkins Hospital. Though the hospital was far from her home, she had to go there because **minorities** were only allowed to seek treatment at certain places. Johns Hopkins was the only place that would serve African American patients at that time due to segregation[5]. Doctors diagnosed her with cancer in 1951. Lacks died six months after her diagnosis, even
20   after **undergoing** cancer treatment. This mother of five children was only 31 years old. Before she died, doctors took cells from her body without her knowledge or permission. A medical procedure for the sampling of cells by rubbing cotton on parts of the body had just been created. This was a new medical practice used in the diagnosis of cancer cells.

[1] trillion (n.) — 1,000,000,000,000
[2] indefinitely (adv.) — without a known ending time
[3] breakthrough (n.) — a new discovery that leads to many other advances
[4] immortal (adj.) — never dying; able to live forever
[5] segregation (n.) — the practice of legally separating people based on their races

This practice would later have **enormous** implications[6] for science. At that time, it was not unusual for doctors to take samples from patients. Patient privacy[7] and widely accepted rules about medical ethics were not in place in those days.

The doctor who originally took Lacks's cells began growing them in a lab. Unlike other cells, her cells were doubling every 24 hours, **generating** new cells. They were named HeLa cells, which takes the first two letters of her first and last name. The doctor began sending her cells to any doctor interested in research. Suddenly, new experiments with these cells became possible and amazing opportunities for research opened up. One of the first breakthroughs was for the polio vaccine[8]. Then just a few short years after Lacks's doctor began freely sharing HeLa cells with other researchers, for-profit **distribution** of the cells began. Companies began mass-producing HeLa cells for commercial gain. By the 1970s, samples of the cells were being sold for $25 per bottle.

The Lacks family did not find out until 1975 that their mother, known only as "HeLa Cells," was famous throughout the scientific community. By this point, HeLa cells were in widespread use all over the world. For perspective, all of the HeLa cells ever used in medical research would weigh 50 billion kilograms and could wrap around the earth three times. However, the Lacks family was so poor that they could not even afford to go to a doctor. When they found out that their mother's cells had been used for years, they called Johns Hopkins Hospital for answers. Nurses and doctors went to the family to draw blood in order to learn more about Henrietta, such as her blood type, in order to study her cells more. The family did not understand the tests, or even really know what cells were. The family thought they were being tested for cancer. They thought their mother was still alive. However, the doctors never got back to them about their "tests." The Lacks family felt they had been taken advantage of by medical professionals.

Though Johns Hopkins has never sold HeLa cells, a number of other companies have. HeLa cells have made some companies and some people very rich. **Nonetheless**, the Lacks family never received any explanation or compensation for their contribution. Rules have since been put in place to make sure doctors can prove that they have **assurance** of patient **consent** for all recommended medical procedures.

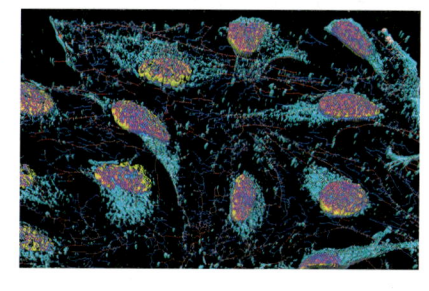

Through studies involving HeLa cells, scientists have made advances in the development of vaccines, drug tests, and cloning. Lacks's cells have also supported research in the fields of space biology, biological supplies, and nanotechnology. Even beyond all of that, Henrietta Lacks's case began a discussion of issues in medicine about patient consent, privacy, and issues related to **ethical** practices still being **debated** today.

---

[6] implication (n.) — an implied or suggested end; a result understood from certain facts
[7] privacy (n.) — the right a person has not to share personal information
[8] vaccine (n.) — medicine given by a shot that stops people from getting a disease in the future

Reading Comprehension

Choose the best answer.

1. Which of the following is true about HeLa cells?
   a. They do not live long outside the body.
   b. They only divide 50 times.
   c. Very few experiments were done using them.
   d. They live indefinitely.

2. What can be inferred about African Americans living in the 1950s from paragraph 2?
   a. They lived closed to hospitals.
   b. Most of them died from cancer.
   c. They did not have adequate access to health services.
   d. The majority of them were farmers.

3. Which of the following is NOT true about HeLa cells?
   a. Johns Hopkins sold the most HeLa sells.
   b. The first breakthrough from using HeLa cells was the vaccine for polio.
   c. The family has never made any money from the use of HeLa cells.
   d. For-profit distribution of the cells began in 1954.

4. What happened in Henrietta Lacks's case?
   a. Lacks was too poor to pay for the cancer tests.
   b. Lacks did not know anyone took her cells.
   c. Johns Hopkins tested Lacks for free because they wanted to try out a new procedure.
   d. Lacks wanted to donate her body to science, but her family would not let her do it.

Paraphrasing Practice

Find the sentence(s) from the given paragraph that means the same as the given sentence. Copy the sentence(s) from the paragraph.

1. **Paragraph 1** Scientists were looking for human cells that could live and divide outside the body, and they finally found them in the 1950s.

   _____

   _____

2. **Paragraph 4** Nurses and doctors drew blood from the family, but the family did not understand what the tests were for.

   _____

   _____

96 Health

Unit 15 Health

Language Focus

When adverbs are used with the present perfect tense, the adverb can appear between the auxiliary verb *have* and the past participle in the verb phrase.

➡ Though Johns Hopkins <u>has</u> *never* <u>sold</u> HeLa cells, a number of other companies have.

➡ Rules <u>have</u> *since* <u>been put in place</u> to make sure doctors can prove that they have assurance of patient consent.

Underline the perfect verb phrase. Circle the adverb if one appears in the sentence.

1. Doctors have been able to grow human cells outside the body since 1907.

2. Unlike some other companies, Johns Hopkins has never sold HeLa cells.

3. Studies involving HeLa cells have helped scientists make breakthroughs in the development of many medicines and medical treatments.

4. Lacks's cells have also supported research in space biology and nanotechnology.

5. In the 1940s and 1950s, African Americans in some US states had not yet won the right to have access to the same health services available to Whites.

Vocabulary Extension

Hint: A common ending for noun word forms is *-ness*.

Complete the chart.

Noun	Verb	Adjective	Adverb
1.	—	enormous	enormously
2.	vary	various	variously
ethics	—	3.	ethically
4.	—	obvious	obviously
medication	—	5.	medically
extraction	6.	extracted	—

Unit 15: An Important Woman in Medicine

Vocabulary Reinforcement

A. Complete the passage using the given words. Three words will NOT be used.

assurance	undergo	consent
debate	distribution	ethical
extraction	medical	enormous

Computers continue to have a(n) **1.** _____ impact on almost every aspect of our lives. These amazing devices have made it much easier for people to work, study, live, and even get **2.** _____ help. Nonetheless, there are issues that we need to consider as more information about our lives and health becomes available online. Not only are there **3.** _____ questions related to what kind of health information can or should be shared online, there are also questions of known and unknown **4.** _____. As more information is uploaded to the internet, individuals have no way of controlling the **5.** _____ of this information with third parties. And even more troubling, there is no **6.** _____ that private information will remain secure with data thieves active worldwide around the clock.

B. Fill in the blanks with the correct phrases. Three phrases will NOT be used.

ethical questions	a different perspective	medical researchers
enormous implications	need assurance	undergoing treatment
distribution of	patient consent	

1. Discovering immortal cells had _____ for future research.

2. There are thousands of cancer patients _____ right now.

3. There were many _____ about the new medical procedure.

4. Now, doctors are required to ask for _____ before performing any tests.

5. Many _____ are working to develop cheap, effective vaccines.

98 Health

Unit 16 Health: Is Your Computer Killing You?

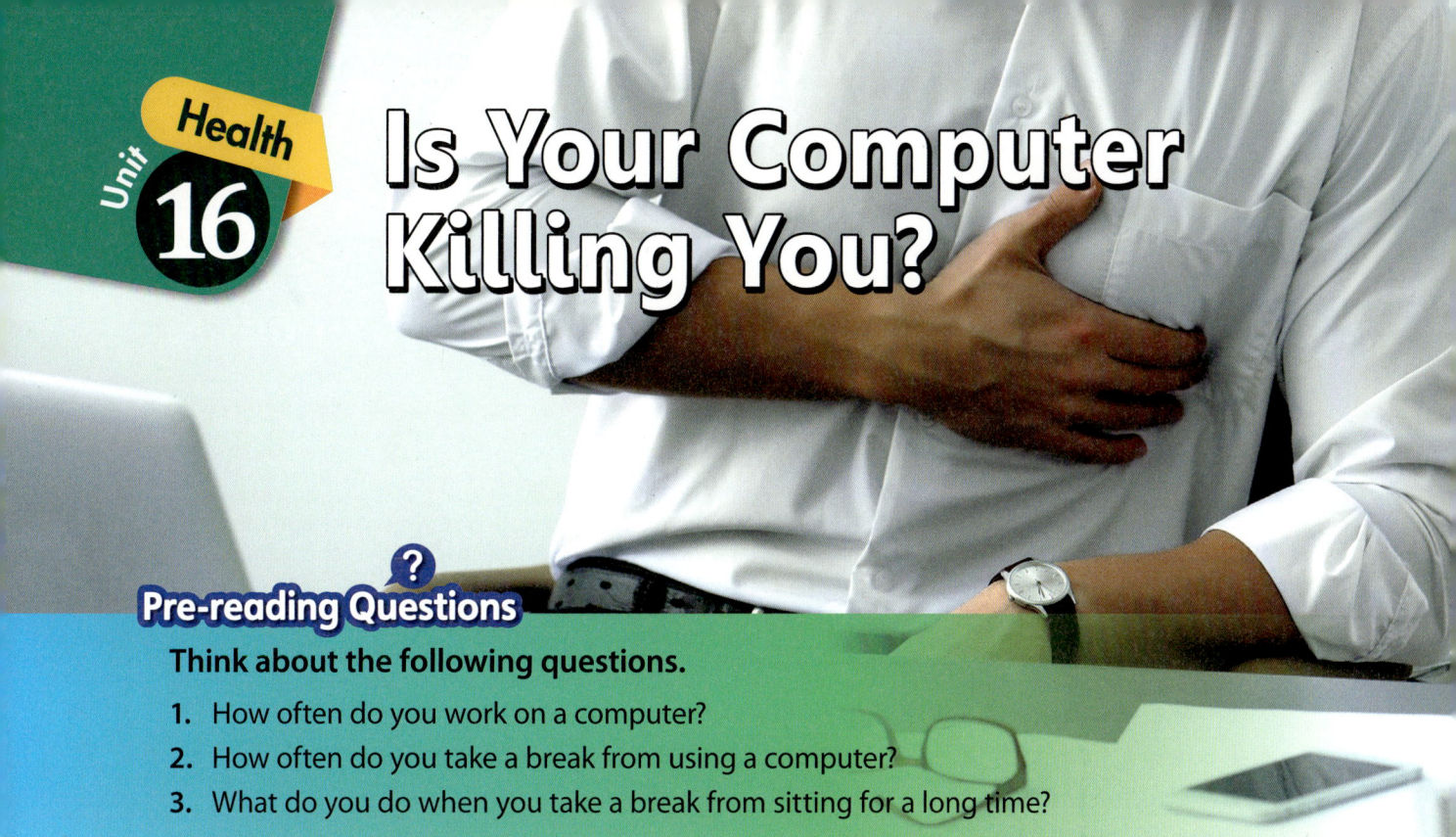

Pre-reading Questions

Think about the following questions.

1. How often do you work on a computer?
2. How often do you take a break from using a computer?
3. What do you do when you take a break from sitting for a long time?

Vocabulary Preview

Write the word that matches the definition.

depression	inherently	monitor	purchase
convert	minimize	pose	mental
tension	shift	occupational	innovation

1. relating to a job or trade — adj. _____
2. to make (something bad) as small as possible — v. _____
3. to buy — v. _____
4. the state of feeling sad, often for no obvious reason — n. _____
5. to move to a different position — v. _____
6. to change to a new form — v. _____
7. a feeling of stress or anxiety — n. _____
8. to cause a danger or damage — v. _____
9. by its basic nature — adv. _____
10. a new idea, device, or method — n. _____
11. related to the mind — adj. _____
12. a device used for showing, watching, or listening to something — n. _____

Health
Too Much Screen Time Does a Body No Good

Topic at a Glance

It is well known that computers have changed the way we all live, work and play. What may not be as obvious is that computers also pose a serious health risk to millions of people. Computer usage can cause back and hand pain and eye strain. People move less and have gained more weight over the computer age. Even relationships and personal lives may suffer. It is important to consider our daily usage of such convenient machines to avoid the dangers of too much screen time.

There is no question that the computer is a valuable tool in our lives. Most people use one every day: a desktop computer, a laptop, a tablet, and a smartphone. In fact, in this day and age, it seems almost impossible to live without computers. But there is a problem. Millions of people who use electronics every day just sit and stare into their screens for long periods of time. It has become quite apparent that there are **occupational** hazards[1] with working on a computer too long, leading to both physical and **mental** issues. Computers could slowly be killing us.

There are various aspects of life that are affected by constantly using computers. Many people who use computers every day suffer from obesity[2] due to sitting too much. Sitting for a long time is actually bad for one's health in many ways and may be killing people. It affects blood circulation[3] and burns very few calories. The link has been made between sitting too much and diabetes[4], heart disease, and cancer. One way to avoid some of the bad effects of sitting too long is to take a break of at least five minutes every hour. Walking and stretching will help reduce some of the pain that results from sitting too much. Some companies are even **converting** a number of their traditional desks to standing desks. Standing desks allow employees to **minimize** the long stretches of their work days spent without getting up from their desks.

Another issue with too much computer usage is pain from poor ergonomics[5]. The daily activities and desk habits of a person can allow certain muscles to become tight and others to become weak over time, leading to injury. One of the easiest ways to relieve **tension** is to get an ergonomic desk and chair and to set **monitors** at eye level, an arm's

---

[1] hazard (n.) — a danger; something that can cause an accident or injury
[2] obesity (n.) — the state of having too much fat in one's body
[3] circulation (n.) — how blood moves through one's body; the movement of a liquid in a closed system
[4] diabetes (n.) — a health problem when one's body can't process carbohydrates well so that there is too much sugar in the blood
[5] ergonomics (n.) — the study of how furniture or equipment can be designed to help people work better

length away from the face. Repeating certain movements day after day may also cause issues, so it is important to pay attention to hands and wrists[6] as well. A good way to avoid injuries to hands and wrists due to computer usage is for a person to **shift** the position of his or her wrists, keep one's arms relaxed, and use the mouse and keyboard lightly.

The computer is a remarkable[7] **innovation** that allows us to do many things at once. In studies related to multitasking[8], researchers have noticed a large increase in ADHD (attention deficit hyperactivity disorder). Not only do more people now seem to need constant stimulation and desire instant gratification[9] from interacting with computers and the internet, but people may be forgetting how to read human emotions. When people rely on too much screen time, they have fewer face-to-face interactions. This may lead to **depression** and other social problems, such as constant unnecessary worry and loneliness. There are now software applications available that allow people to set up time limits for their internet or computer usage. These programs force people to look up from the screen or stop working at regular intervals. Another tip is to seek out social interaction during a work break.

Eye problems and headaches from overuse of computers are additional physical issues that affect many people. Such problems should not be ignored. Computer screens require that people move their eyes back and forth[10] across a screen very quickly. Many also look from a bright screen to papers on their desk, which requires a lot of effort for their eyes to quickly adjust. Bright computer screens can also damage parts inside eyes. Doctors recommend the 20-20-20 rule: look at things 20 feet away for 20 seconds after looking at a screen for 20 minutes.

Blue light insomnia[11] is yet another danger of too much computer usage. Light from computer screens can cause one's body to produce less of a chemical that regulates sleep. Blue light from a screen tricks the brain into believing it is seeing light from the sun. This throws off the natural sleep-wake cycle of the body. In order to avoid insomnia, **purchase** blue-blocking glasses to wear or avoid looking at screens at night.

Computers are not **inherently** bad; however, many people cannot go a single day without one. In order to avoid the harmful effects **posed** by too much computer usage, people need to make the choice to step away from the computer, put the phone down, and make plans with friends. Taking frequent breaks to stretch and exercising certainly won't hurt either.

---

[6] wrist (n.) — the part of one's arm just above the hand
[7] remarkable (adj.) — amazing; worthy of note
[8] multitasking (n.) — the act of doing several jobs all at the same time
[9] gratification (n.) — the state of receiving satisfaction or pleasure
[10] back and forth (adv. phr.) — from one side to the other side
[11] insomnia (n.) — a medical problem which makes it hard for a person to sleep

Reading Comprehension

Choose the best answer.

1. Which of the following is NOT true according to paragraph 2?
   a. Circulation may be poor from overuse of computers.
   b. It is important to take a five-minute break for every hour of sitting.
   c. Many people who use computers sit too much.
   d. There is no link between sitting too much and life span.

2. Why does the author mention poor ergonomics?
   a. Bad posture results in a lack of productivity.
   b. It is a common cause of work-related injuries.
   c. It is an effective way to relax the legs while typing.
   d. Most people cannot afford an ergonomic desk and chair.

3. According to paragraph 4, all of the following are true EXCEPT
   a. People crave instant gratification.
   b. Researchers have seen an increase in ADHD.
   c. Computers pose a greater health risk than smoking.
   d. Too much screen time can lead to loneliness.

4. What is the problem with blue light?
   a. It tricks the brain to become sleepy.
   b. It can cause insomnia.
   c. It is not bright enough to see.
   d. It regulates the motion of one's eyes.

Paraphrasing Practice

Find the sentence(s) from the given paragraph that means the same as the given sentence. Copy the sentence(s) from the paragraph.

1. **Paragraph 3** Feelings of physical stress can be relieved by arranging computer monitors at the correct height and by using an appropriate chair and desk.

   _____

   _____

2. **Paragraph 6** Blue light disrupts the natural cycle of when a person sleeps and wakes.

   _____

   _____

Unit 16 Health

Language Focus

The word *there* can serve as a dummy subject in a sentence. It is followed by some form of *be* which matches in number the real subject of the sentence.

➡ There *is* a link between sitting too much and certain health problems.
➡ There *are* occupational hazards with working on a computer too long.

Choose the correct form of *be* to complete each sentence.

1. There (is / are) many aspects of life that are affected by constantly using computers.

2. There (is / are) no question that the computer is a valuable tool in our lives.

3. There (is / are) now software applications that allow people to limit their computer usage.

4. There (is / are) some benefit to taking short breaks from computer work, even just five minutes per hour.

5. There (is / are) another danger of too much computer usage called blue light insomnia.

Vocabulary Extension

Read the dictionary definitions below. Find the words in the Vocabulary Preview list on page 99 that match these definitions.

1. _____	*verb (used with an object)* 1. to change (something) into a different form or properties; to transform. 2. to cause to adopt a different religion, political belief, opinion, etc.; 3. to turn to another or a particular use or purpose; 4. to modify (something) so as to serve a different function; 5. to obtain an equivalent value for in an exchange or calculation, as money or units of measurement. *verb (used without an object)* 6. to become changed or turned. *noun* 7. one who has been changed, as to a religion or opinion.
2. _____	*verb (used with an object)* 1. to acquire by the payment of money; to buy. 2. to acquire by effort or sacrifice. 3. to be sufficient to buy. *noun* 4. acquisition by the payment of money; buying, or a single act of buying. 5. something that is bought. 6. a firm grip or footing on something.
3. _____	*noun* 1. a person appointed to supervise students, applicants, etc., taking an examination, chiefly to prevent cheating. 2. a device for observing, detecting, or recording the operation of a machine or system, especially an automatic control system. 3. an instrument for detecting something dangerous. *verb (used with an object)* 4. to listen or view in order to check the quality of something. 5. to observe, record, or detect with instruments that have no effect upon the operation or condition. 6. to oversee, supervise, or regulate. 7. to watch closely or check continually. *verb (used without an object)* 8. to serve as a detector, supervisor, etc.

Vocabulary Reinforcement

A. Complete the passage using the given words. Three words will NOT be used.

posed	mental	innovation
depression	inherently	monitors
purchasing	converts	minimized

Small companies in which employees work long hours in front of computer 1. _____ may not be able to afford standing desks or ergonomic chairs for everyone. But there are some cheap ways to avoid employee health issues 2. _____ by long hours of computer usage. An easy office 3. _____ might be to schedule "meeting walks." For small teams, this is a great way to meet about projects and get some exercise at the same time. 4. _____ some green plants for the office is another cheap way to fight employee 5. _____. Research shows that seeing plants gives people a 6. _____ lift and makes their blood pressure drop.

B. Fill in the blanks with the correct phrases. Three phrases will NOT be used.

relieve tension	purchase a new monitor	remarkable innovations
minimize the risk	convert light to energy	lead to depression
inherently bad	occupational hazards	

1. Some jobs are more physical than a desk job and have many _____.

2. I like to get a massage in order to _____ because my neck gets very tight.

3. Not talking to people can sometimes _____.

4. The black panels on top of the office building _____ and help lower the company's electric bill.

5. The computer has been one of the most _____ in history.

Appendix

A list of useful prefixes and suffixes

Prefix	Meaning	Word	Other forms
ad-	to(ward)	advance, advertise	a-, ab-, ac-, af-, ag-, al-, an-, ap-, aq-, ar-, as-, at-
com-	with	complicated, confuse	co-, col-, con-, cor-
de-	down, away	describe, deduct	
dis-	not	dislike	
dis-	apart, away	distance	di-, dif-
ex-	out, beyond	express	e-, ef-
ex-	former	ex-president	
in-	not	inconsistent	ig-, il-, im-, ir-
in-	in(to)	instruct	il-, im-, ir-
inter-	between, among	internet	
mis-	wrong(ly)	mishear, mistreat	
non-	not	nonstick, nonsmoking	
ob-	against	oppose	o-, oc-, of-, op-
ob-	to(ward)	obtain	o-, oc-, of-, op-
over-	above	overtired, overcook	
pre-	before	predict	
pro-	forward	progress	
pro-	in favour of	pro-life	
re-	back, again	rearrange, redraw	
sub-	under	support, subscribe	suc-, suf-, sug-, sum-, sur-, sus-
trans-	across, beyond	transfer	tra-, tran-
un-	not	unable	

Suffix	Meaning / Function	Word	Other forms
-ance	the condition of; the result of / to make a noun	assistance, attendance	-ancy, -ence, -ency
-tion		estimation, generation	-ion, -sion
-ism		capitalism, nationalism	
-ity		diversity, maturity	
-logy		biology, psychology	
-ment		achievement, requirement	
-ness		carelessness, sweetness	
-ship		citizenship, friendship	
-an	a person of; one who does / to make a noun (person)	American, Korean	-ian
-ant		assistant, participant	-ent
-ee		employee, referee	
-er		banker, painter	-ar, -or
-ist		biologist, guitarist	
-able	being; having the property of / to make an adjective	honorable, portable	-ible
-al		natural, visual	
-ant		relevant, significant	
-ary		military, voluntary	
-ent		evident, sufficient	
-ous		courageous, malicious	
-y		noisy, sleepy	
-ful	full of / to make an adjective	careful, helpful	
-ic	like; having the nature of; related to / to make an adjective	metallic, symbolic	
-ish		childish, girlish	
-ive		effective, supportive	
-less	without / to make an adjective	fearless, tasteless	
-er	having more of / to make a comparative adjective	bigger, slower	
-est	having the most of / to make a superlative adjective	biggest, slowest	
-ly	in the manner of / to make an adverb	carelessly, logically	
-ate	to make / to make a verb	disintegrate, estimate	
-en		blacken, deepen	
-fy		clarify, unify	
-ize		memorize, organize	

How to Use the App

1. Scan the QR code at the back of the book.

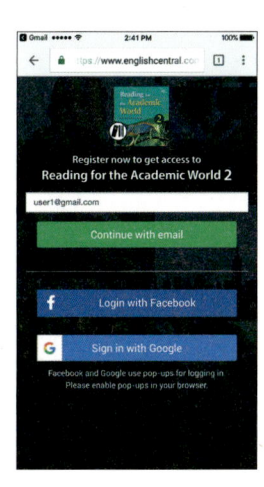

2. Type your email address. Then click on "Continue with email."

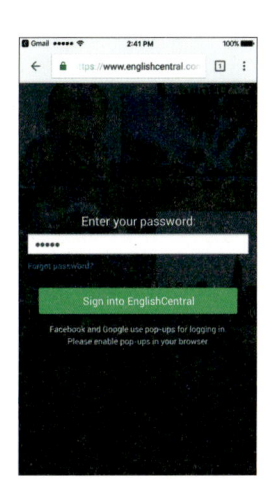

3a. If you already have an EnglishCentral account, enter your password.

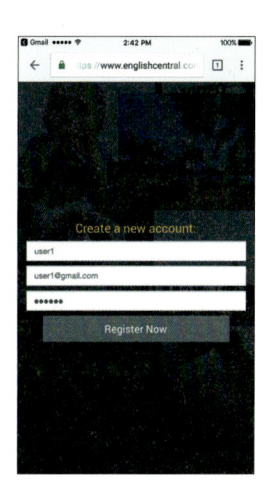

3b. If you don't have an EnglishCentral account, add your name, email, and password. Then click on "Register Now."

4. You now have the textbook course in your account. Click on "START."

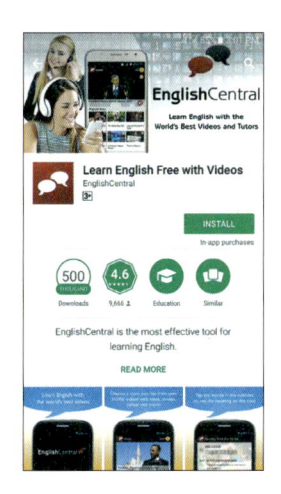

5. Install the EnglishCentral app.

6. Click on "Sign In." Sign in with the email address that you used in #2.

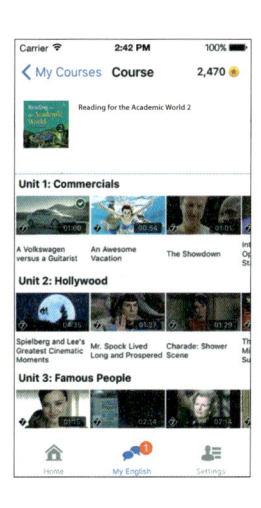

7. You will see your textbook course when you log in. Complete all the units to finish the course.